FURTHER, FASTER, TOGETHER

GODLY ADVICE TO FOSTER A DEEPER, LONG LASTING, AND MEANINGFUL RELATIONSHIP.

KENNETH D. PHELPS

Copyright © 2016 by KENNETH D. PHELPS

FURTHER, FASTER, TOGETHER
GODLY ADVICE TO FOSTER A DEEPER, LONG LASTING, AND MEANINGFUL RELATIONSHIP.
by KENNETH D. PHELPS

Printed in the United States of America
Edited by Xulon Press.

ISBN 9781498458955

All rights reserved solely by the author. The author guarantees all contents are original and do not infringe upon the legal rights of any other person or work. No part of this book may be reproduced in any form without the permission of the author. The views expressed in this book are not necessarily those of the publisher.

Unless otherwise indicated, Scripture quotations are taken from the the King James Version (KJV) – *public domain.*

Scripture quotations taken from the Holy Bible, New International Version (NIV). Copyright © 1973, 1978, 1984, 2011 by Biblica, Inc.™. Used by permission. All rights reserved.

Scripture quotations taken from the New King James Version (NKJV). Copyright © 1982 by Thomas Nelson, Inc. Used by permission. All rights reserved.

Scripture quotations taken from the Living Bible (TLB). Copyright © 1971 by Tyndale House Foundation. Used by permission of Tyndale House Publishers Inc., Carol Stream, Illinois 60188. All rights reserved.

Scripture quotations taken from the The New Testament: An Expanded Translation by Kenneth D. Wuest, 1961. Reprinted 1994. Used by Permission. All rights reserved.

Cover, rear and author photo taken by: Audrey Hord/ Audrey Hord Photography LLC, 2015

All rights reserved. No part of this publication may be reproduced, stored in a retrieval system, or transmitted in any form or by any means—electronic, mechanical, photocopying, recording, or otherwise—without the prior written permission of the publisher or Imani Faith Productions/Imani Faith Publishing. The only exception is brief quotations in printed reviews. This manuscript is the property of IMANI Faith Productions. Please do not duplicate or share without permission from IMANI or Dr. Kenneth D. Phelps.

www.kennethdphelps.com

www.xulonpress.com

Table of Contents

Introduction/Prolegomena vii
The Goal..x
Dedication xiii
Acknowledgements xv
Endorsements xix

ONE
I've Got to Get Myself Together 23

TWO
Friendship..43

THREE
Equally Yoked! 57

FOUR
Cut Ungodly Soul Ties!...79

FIVE
Become Relationship Custodians...87

SIX
Exit Strategy 95

SEVEN
Let's Stay Together 102

EIGHT
Forgiveness—The Greatest Gift 110

FINAL THOUGHTS 121
ABOUT THE AUTHOR 125
APPENDIX A 129
NOTES 133

INTRODUCTION

PROLEGOMENA

I started my theological education at Northern Baptist Theological Seminary in the fall of 1994. The first book that I read, in my Introduction to Theology class, was *Christian Faith, An Introduction to the Study of Faith*[1], by Hendrikus Berkhof. I vividly remember eagerly opening my course book and reading two words, "Introduction" and "Prolegomena." I thought to myself, "Prolegomena? What in the world have I gotten myself into?" I had never heard the word prolegomena and had no idea what it meant; I remember feeling overwhelmed and defeated from the start. I remember calling my Theology professor, Dr. Douglas Sharp, sharing my fears and inquiring, "What does prolegomena mean?" He laughed and said, "Ken, it means first things first." Then he took a moment to be very pastoral and assured me, "One day, I'm going to make you a theologian!" With the help of Dr. Sharp, I was able to push past my ignorance and get through the Introduction to Theology course, and ultimately achieve my M.Div. degree at Northern. However, I am still waiting on Dr. Sharp to make good on his promise and make me a theologian.

As I embark on this journey to write a relationship book, I do so with fear and much apprehension; and feeling pretty much like I felt over twenty years ago at Northern Seminary, questioning, "What have I gotten myself into?"

As I write this book, marriages are on the decline. Most people are simply deciding not to get married and for those that do,[2] most demographers conclude that, "fifty percent of all marriages [will] fail." [3]

Not only are marriages under attack, but also our families: children are at odds with their parents and parents are at odds with their children. Additionally, brothers and sisters don't get along. The family is under satanic attack. The truth is, most people are having relationship issues. In knowing that relationships are in such dire straits, I feel totally inadequate to write a manual on helping individuals find better ways to communicate their hopes of creating and maintaining meaningful and lasting relationships.

Therefore, when I started thinking, "Why should **I** write this book?" the Holy Spirit said, "Why not you?" He began to remind me that although I have been formally educated, receiving several

Introduction

degrees from undergraduate to graduate—secular to divinity—it is not my education that qualifies me. I've been preaching the gospel since 1990 and pastoring Concord Missionary Baptist Church for twenty-one years at the time of writing this book. Again, the Holy Spirit reminded me that pastoring is not what qualifies me to write this book. Ultimately, I am qualified because of my relational experiences; that is my relational failures. What qualifies me to write this book is what I have been through and, more importantly, what I have survived!

In fact, it is revelations gained from my mistakes that make me overly qualified to write this book! My success in relationships and life were birthed out of my mistakes. My failures were, are, and continue to be the source and substance for each chapter of this book.

ORGANIZATION OF THIS BOOK

Further, Faster, Together focuses on things to consider before committing to marriage. The book was inspired by the relationship tips series that I preached at the Concord Missionary Baptist Church. Each sermon in the series was the skeleton for each chapter. They have all been re-written for print and seasoned with real life stories.

The names in most cases have been changed to protect the identity of those involved.

At the end of each chapter is a set of discussion and reflection questions and /or an application component designed to enable you to practice the principles outlined in the chapter. Reflection and application is key to your going further, faster together.

THE GOAL

The goal of *Further, Faster, Together,* is to equip the reader with some battle tested relationship tips that have been saturated and seasoned with the Word of God; to produce healthier relationships, for God's glory. It is the strategy of Satan to attack and weaken the church and our communities through creating broken relationships. Satan knows that if he can weaken/destroy the family or our critical core relationships, (i.e. marriages, friendships and romantic love interests), he can weaken and destroy the community, the church, or the kingdom of God. He knows that if he can get us to fight against each other, or better yet, operate in sin, ignorance and unforgiveness, the people of God will live defeated and devastated lives. We must never forget that, "we wrestle not against flesh and blood, but against principalities, against powers, against the rulers of the darkness of

Introduction

this world, against spiritual wickedness in high places" (Eph. 6:12). Satan wants us to think that those we are in a relationship with are the enemy, when in fact they are not; even if you feel like they are! Satan is a deceiver (Rev. 20:10) and a liar (John 8:44). He is "like" a roaring lion seeking whom he can devour. (1 Peter 5:8)

The remedy is for the church to foster and encourage healthy "Christ" centered, biblically based, relationships. It is my belief that strong relationships build strong churches and communities. *Further, Faster, Together* is a book designed to help encourage healthy "Christ" centered relationships, for the glory of God. It is my prayer that after reading this book and applying the principles therein, you will experience healthy and productive relationships that will help fulfill your God given purpose and destiny.

DEDICATION

The Phelps Family; L-R David, Veneeta, and Morgan. Kenneth (Not Pictured)

THANK YOU

I am eternally indebted to so many.

Let me begin by thanking those who are often the last mentioned, but to whom I am most indebted: My darling wife and best friend, Veneeta and my children, Morgan, David, and Kenneth. Without your unconditional support, love and sacrifice, this book would not have been possible.

To my heroes: my Mom, the late Mary Marzette and Dad, the late Kenneth W. Phelps, thank you for giving me life and the tools to live.

To my Mother-in-Law and late Father in Law: Mother Annie Brewster and Deacon Dan Brewster thank you for showing me the way. Great is your faithfulness.

To my family: Uncle James and Aunt Vivian Robinson, Aunt Donna and Uncle Book Felton, Uncle Willie and Aunt Laura Merkerson, and Aunt Rosalyn and Uncle Casanova Richardson, thank you for your love and support. To all my God-parents: Johnny and Joyce Jackson, Virgil and Gwen Fleming and Bernard and the late Carol Porter. My Sisters and brothers: Virginia Brewster, Tasha Merritt (Kenney), Herbert Jackson, Michelle Pettis, Sharyn Felton, Lesa Felton, Derek Felton (Vikki), Donald Montgomery (Paris), Jessie Turner (Cleaster), Monique Porter, Yvette Porter-Steele (Redd) and all my God-children, thank you for being there.

To my Spiritual mentors in the ministry: Rev. James and Gladys Fair, Rev. Dr. M.E. Saunders, Rev. Dr. U.A. Hughey, Rev. William H. Conley and Bishop Michael F. Mack, and my Spiritual Sisters and Brothers: Bishop Simon Gordon, Bishop William Hudson III, Pastor James T. Meeks, Pastor Clarence and Lady Shauntia Stowers, Pastor Christopher T. and Lady JoJo Harris, Pastor Corey Brooks, Pastor Charles and Dr. Tara Jenkins, Dr. Tasha Brown, Apostle Donald and Lady Gloria Alford, Rev. Norman and Diane Donahue, Rev. Dr. Michael Noble, Rev. Dr. J.C. Smith, Rev. Dr. Steven D. and Helen Lewis, Rev. Vincent and Gina Lewis, Rev. Ferlander and Janice Lewis, Rev. Eugene and Claudia Ellington, Rev. Steven and Karla Greer, Rev. Steven D. and Lesa Holloway, Rev. Dr. Jesse and Rev. Coral Brown, Rev. Krista Alston, Rev. Darius and Deborah Brooks and Rev. Dr. Craig M. Smith, thanks for giving me the ministry blueprint.

Thank You

To my companions in the gospel, and sons and daughters in the ministry, who are far too many to name, thank you for going on this journey with me.

To my Facebook family, who inspired the relationship tips teaching series: Loletha Stubbs, Felicia Harvey, Charlese Gary, Allan Day, Nichelle "Ne-Ne" Harvey, Nicole Gardner, Kendall Harvey, Kimberly England, Min. Katrena Mathews, Natasha Martin, Kimberly "Redd" Stubbs, Tatianna Knight, Polly Jo Chalstrom, Sheldon Lane and few others, thank you.

To my editor, Terralyn Frazier (The Write Approach). Thank you for your due diligence, feedback and contribution to make this book a much better product.

To my Imani Faith Productions staff and all those who participated in the "Read a Round" and proofreading of each chapter. Thank you for your feedback and support.

To my attorney and accountant Donald Montgomery, thank you for your wise counsel.

To my publisher, Xulon Press and support staff, thank you for all your hard work and the professional publishing assistance. Thank you for helping to make my dream a reality.

To the members of the Concord Missionary Baptist Church, thank you for your unconditional love and support. This book is dedicated to you.

To my Concord Community Organization (CCO) Board of Directors, I am so excited about our future. Thank you for believing in my vision and me.

To all those whose names were not mentioned, but whose contributions and acts of love and kindness during this season of my life are so noted; Thank you. You have made a very difficult journey bearable.

Finally, thanks be to God, which giveth us the victory through our Lord Jesus Christ. (1 Cor. 15:57)

ENDORSEMENTS

"I am honored to share with you that in this book [*Further, Faster, Together*], Dr. Phelps taps into the gem of human sustainability as he unapologetically discusses the lack of core competencies in modern day relationships.

The combination of life experience, education, and spiritual wisdom rings thunderously as he not only gives us direction, but also supports our journey toward improving our lives.

His poignant positions, and healthy directives, sprinkled with the grace and care of a pastor gives hope to every reader. The question of our existence and the hope of our very moments loudly celebrate this fact that Dr. Phelps shares with us; the fact is that we can survive.

I'm encourage with this writing because in it I see that we clearly can go further, faster, together; and enjoy every minute of it.
Take this trip with me and journey through these pages with Dr. Phelps because life, is about to get better for all of us."

-Bishop Simon Gordon
Tried Stone FGB Church

"'Teamwork makes the dream work' is not just a fancy phrase; it's an honest truth that reminds us that a steady pace and great productivity are tied to healthy relationships. This book [*Further,*

Faster, Together] is a relational resource for those who seek to make meaningful progress in all lanes of life."

Charles Jenkins
FellowshipChicago.com

"I have always appreciated Pastor Kenneth David Phelps fresh insight on familiar issues. In *Further, Faster, Together,* he writes with clarity and crispness; always grounded in the Scriptures. I love it! He backs it up with the Book! Again in this masterpiece he has given all who read this a chance to grow and mature. I congratulate him again. This is a must read for all pastors, counselors, and ministry leaders who are serious about strengthening the bonds in the fellowship. Thank you again, my colleague and friend."

-Rev. Dr. Craig Melvin Smith,
Freedom Baptist Church

"If you only read one book on relationships, make it *Further, Faster, Together* by Dr. Kenneth D. Phelps. Phelps hit the nail on the head! A must read for those seeking practical biblically based counsel on how to improve their relationship. Whether your relationship needs a minor tune up or major over haul, this book is for you!"

-Pastor Corey B. Brooks
New Beginnings Church

"'In this age of 'Facebook friends' that you don't even know, Dr. Ken Phelps understands how to become a *'good'* friend as the foundation for all lasting relationships, especially family and marriage. His transparent approach emphasizing the forgiveness of God, yourself, and significant others is the need of the hour!"

-Dr. Robert "Bob" Price
Northern Seminary
Associate Professor of Evangelism and Urban Ministry

Endorsements

"Dr. Phelps has done a wonderful job of providing practical recommendations for navigating relationships. Dr. Phelps just doesn't provide you with relationship advice, he gives tools and resources for understanding how to make your relationships work. Relying on the Word of God, Phelps offers proven methods that will bring relationship success to all those who read his book. I highly recommend it!"

-Rev. Dr. Tasha Vinson Brown
Galewood Community Church United Church of Christ
Northern Seminary
Director of Urban Relations and Adjunct
Professor of Spiritual Development

"Kenneth Phelps has done the Church a tremendous service in this phenomenal work, *Further, Faster, Together*. These biblical principles on building and nurturing healthy relationships will be a blessing for years to come. Thank God for his insight."

-Dr. James C. Perkins, Pastor
Greater Christ Baptist Church Detroit, Michigan
President, Progressive National Baptist Convention Inc.

"A tremendous resource that demonstrates the love, commitment, compassion, tenacity, and willingness to connect to another person in order to build a long lasting relationship. Dr. Phelps has written a compelling and insightful body of work with strong biblical truths to substantiate the relationship tips provided within its pages. This book also reminded me of the important role that both forgiveness and trust play in the process of fostering successful relationships. *Further, Faster, Together* provides a wonderful model for navigating the complex challenges encountered while establishing relationships."

-Bishop William Hudson III
Prayer & Faith Outreach Ministries
Coadjutor Bishop of the Pilgrim Assemblies International

"Are you looking to strengthen your relationships? Do you desire to go deeper with those who mean the most to you? Being relationally rich is just as important as being financially rich. If you are in a relationship or plan to be in one in the future, *Further, Faster, Together* is a brilliantly written relationship tip book by Dr. Kenneth D Phelps. It offers real authentic solutions steeped in the word of God, with practical wisdom and application. *Further, Faster, Together* is a new literary gem for the Body of Christ. It provides an excellent roadmap for couples to go further, faster together!"

-Clarence E Stowers
Senior Pastor, Mars Hill Baptist Church of Chicago

"Hats off to Dr. Kenneth D. Phelps, D. Min., a preacher with the rare ability to keep his eyes fixed on heaven and his feet planted on earth. Thank you for allowing God to use you to bring us a wealth of practical knowledge, and revelatory teaching, all centered on the Word of God infused with experiences from your life. This book captures a glimpse of the types of relationships we deal with on daily basis, and gives us strategies to make them better!"

-Darla Steele
Co-Pastor, Grace Church Ministries, Inc.

Columbia, South Carolina

ONE

I've Got to Get Myself Together

Romans 7:14–21

"Yesterday I was clever, so I wanted to change the world.

Today I am wise, so I am changing myself."

— Rumi

RELATIONSHIP TIP #1:

"The starting point of any relationship is YOU. If YOU are messed up and out of control, YOU are already operating in a relational deficit!"

The substratum or foundation of all relationships is YOU. For years when I had problems in my relationship with others, I would pray for them. I would ask God to fix them, I mean the problem had to be them, because it could not possibly be me! Here's what I learned, when God wanted to "fix" my relationship at home, church or work, he usually did not start with them. He started with me. God changed the relationship, by first changing me! So now when there is an issue in my relationships at church, home or the workplace, I pray a different prayer. I now pray like this: Search me Lord. If you find anything in me that is not of thee, please remove it. Fix me Lord! Fix me! "Create in me a clean heart, O God, and renew a right spirit within me." (Ps. 51:10)[4]

First God changes my thinking (and my attitude) and then He changes my behavior. Ghandi was right, ultimately, we have to be or become the change we want to see in our world. Transformation in your world begins and ends with you. It is important that you and I do not conform to this world, but be transformed by the renewing of our minds, so that we may discern the good, acceptable and perfect will of God for our lives. (Rom. 12:2)

Beloved, you cannot change anybody except yourself. If you want transformation in your life, you must submit to God's transforming power to change your life and others will follow!

The self[5] by its very nature is undisciplined. The self needs constant discipline that is: temperance, self-control, or self-leadership. Yet self-discipline is a struggle for most people. If we are honest with ourselves most of us are OC (out of control) most of the time!

Although according to the word of God, we are to live by, walk in, and be led by the Spirit; but most of us live by, walk in, and are led by our flesh! Here are some things to ponder about the flesh:

- *Our flesh makes us say things we should not!*
- *Our flesh makes us eat things we should not!*
- *Our flesh makes us think things we should not!*
- *Our flesh makes us go places we should not!*

Let's be honest. Have you ever gone somewhere you knew you should not have gone? Your mind and your spirit were saying, "You should not go there! We should not be doing this!" But the flesh is saying, "Come on, it will be fun!"

Lack of self-discipline can also be applied to relationships. It is possible to be relationally OC (out of control). We have all been attracted to that which is not good for us. I know I have many times. It took God to deliver me out of those situations, because I did not have the mind or will power to let them go. I promised God that if He delivered me, I would never go back there again! But the problem is, my flesh didn't agree to or sign up for that plan! At the first available opportunity, my flesh would lead me right back into what God had already delivered me from! I usually went back to that place with a greater degree of attraction and propensity for emotional destruction; and the need for deliverance would begin again. I thank God for His grace and mercy and that He loved me enough not to give up on me.

The truth is we all have seasons in our lives, where we are simply out of control!

In Romans 7:14–21 Paul describes the spiritual/moral internal conflict in this passage of scripture:

"I know that God's standards are spiritual, but I have a corrupt nature, sold as a slave to sin. I don't realize what I'm doing. I don't do what I want to do. Instead, I do what I hate. I don't do what I want to do, but I agree that God's standards are good. So I am no longer the one who is doing the things I hate, but sin that lives in me is doing them. I know that nothing good lives in me; that is, nothing good lives in my corrupt nature. Although I have the desire to do what is right, I don't do it. I don't do the good I want to do. Instead, I do the evil that I don't want to do. Now, when I do what I don't want to do, I am no longer the one who is doing it. Sin that lives in me is doing it." Rom. 7:14–17 God's Word Translation

My interpretation of what Paul is saying is: I know that God's laws are supernatural and divinely inspired, but I am naughty by nature. Although I know the Word of God, I can be dirty, unethical, immoral, lustful and sometimes nasty. I am out of control, beyond bipolar, more like schizophrenic most of the time. I don't do what I want to do, that's why I agree that God's Word is good and necessary. So I am no longer the one who is doing the things I hate, but sin that lives in me is doing them.

By his own testimony, Paul is saying, as great as I am, I have some crazy moments in my life. And Paul is not alone. We too are imperfect human beings and there is a little something wrong with all of us. None of us are perfect, except God! There is an oft-heard maxim in the recovery community that holds true in this instance: "We're as sick as our secrets."[6] We have all had moments in our lives, where we've felt like Paul—you really want to do the right thing, but you end up doing the wrong thing. We all have done or said something that we said we would never do! Paul is suggesting, that every now and then, he's out of control and therefore, must get himself together. It is that truth and reality that we must grasp. Before engaging in any relationship with others, it is important to get yourself together. When you put time and energy into creating the best possible you, everything else will naturally fall into place.

Therefore, initially, your main focus has to be on becoming the best "self" possible for the benefit of any relationship. This point of view is not narcissistic, selfish or self-centered. Moreover, it should be considered as self-discipline.

Let me take this moment to describe the various components of one's self or "the self." There are many ways to define and describe the self and the components thereof. For purposes of this chapter, I would like to describe the self in terms of the emotional, financial, physical and spiritual self and the extensions thereof. I have chosen these components; because in my experience and opinion, they along with the cognitive self, need to be healthy and intact before pursuing relationship with others. Let us first consider the emotional component of the self.

Emotional Self:

The Merriam-Webster Dictionary Online, defines emotions as the "affective aspect of consciousness: feeling. A state of feeling. A conscious mental reaction (as anger or fear) subjectively experienced as strong feeling usually directed toward a specific object and typically accompanied by physiological and behavioral changes in the body" [7]

To demonstrate how destructive or dangerous uncontrolled emotions can be in a relationship, if not dealt with properly, let's consider the case of John and Carol.

John and Carol met online. John was an out of work veteran, who had served two tours in Afghanistan. Carol was a schoolteacher. Both were lonely and looking for companionship. They began chatting online via Facebook. This went on for a few months. They decided to take the relationship to the next level and meet face to face. At first things were great between John and Carol, but eventually John became possessive and argumentative. Finally Carol saw their arguments as a sign that they weren't compatible and broke up with John.

The breakup really hurt John. He decided to go to the Veterans Administration (VA) Hospital for counseling. As a part of John's initial processing at the VA, John was given a battery of physical and emotional tests. One of them was the 360 Degree Feedback process.[8] During the 360 Degree Feedback process, John discovered that most of the people around him found him to be argumentative and difficult to deal with. This result was consistent with Carol's experience. The doctors eventually diagnosed John with PTSD (Post Traumatic Stress Disorder). Once he started the regimen of counseling and medication, John's emotional health dramatically improved. John was a much better person to be around. Eventually he and Carol began to date again.

John is not alone. In my personal observation, people today seem to be more emotional and on the edge. Perhaps it is because they are emotionally out of control, mad, angry, or even violent; while others, are simply depressed.

That is why I strongly recommend that before getting into a relationship you make sure you are emotionally healthy. Both parties have to be seasoned and emotionally ready for a relationship. Oftentimes this involves letting go of past issues and relationships and moving on. One must have the courage to confront and conquer their emotional issues, insecurities, and failed relationships, before engaging in a new relationship.

Emotions are also tied to our maturity level. My definition of immaturity is simply, "Not ready. Premature. Before its time." On the other hand, I define maturity as "being grown up or ready." Most relationships fail, because they happen prematurely and they don't have what it needs or what it takes to survive.

Therefore, before embarking into a relationship you need to make sure that you are emotionally ready to commit to the "process." One of the best barometers for this is in our ability or inability to commit.

RELATIONSHIP TIP #2:

"Lack of commitment is another sign of immaturity. Quit committing to those that cannot, nor ever will, commit to you. If there is no future or commitment, then you may be wasting your time."

The following story is a great example of what could happen if you commit to a person who is not ready to emotionally commit to you.

Everyone thought Tim and Kris would make a great couple. Both were in their mid-thirties, educated, Christian and were well established in their careers. Neither one had ever been married nor had kids. They finally agreed to go out on a date. They found they had a lot in common. The only problem was, Tim wanted to get married and have a child, while Kris preferred to keep her options open. Tim and Kris were at different stages or levels of commitment in the relationship, which made the relationship stressful at times. They dated on an off for a while, but eventually decided to go their separate ways.

Emotional health and maturity plays a vital role in any relationship and therefore should be given your utmost attention. Now let's consider the financial self.

Financial Self

RELATIONSHIP TIP #3:

"In relationships MONEY Matters."

Money is important because it informs our self-worth (self-esteem) and net worth. I learned in my high school consumer education class that money is important because it determines what we can and cannot do. Money gives you freedom and choices. Let's consider Joe and Tammy's story.

Tammy and Joe grew up together and eventually started dating. They had unprotected sex and Tammy became pregnant. Tammy and Joe cared very deeply for each other and decided to move in together. They had a few more children together. After the third child Tammy became frustrated with Joe, because he would not propose to her. Finally, he informed Tammy that the reason that he didn't want to get married, was because he did not have the money. He didn't have the money for a wedding or to consistently provide for a wife and family.

The preceding example demonstrates how money can impact a relationship and even prevent it from going to the next level.

Unfortunately, when it comes to relationships, money matters. I find financial issues or "money matters" to be in the top five issues that most couples struggle with, because our sense of self is tied to our net-worth and buying power. He or she who has or makes the most money, usually controls the money and the relationship. Most people understand that, which is why they prefer to have "their own" money; because for them, financial freedom equals relational freedom!

Therefore, in preparation for a relationship, individuals must get their personal finances in check. This involves getting your spending and debt under control (if possible eliminate debt), before getting into a relationship with someone. Financial health helps you to be an asset to any relationship you choose to pursue. After you have gotten your emotional and financial self in check, the next component to consider is your physical self.

Physical Self

The physical component of the self focuses on the body. This involves physical appearance, fitness, and health. It has often been said, looks are not everything (and it is not) or you can't judge a book by its cover. However, humans are visual beings and what we see matters. In fact, first impressions are often lasting impressions.

That is why it is important to always make a good first impression, because you may not ever get a second chance.

Appearance is important because it is how you look or appear to others. It is critical that when others see you, that they see the best you possible. This involves being well groomed and manicured. When you are dressed up, you feel better about yourself. My Mom once gave me a great piece of advice concerning appearance, preaching, and self-esteem, she said, "Always dress well when preaching. The better you look to people, the better you will sound to people. And more important, the better you look, the better you will feel about yourself." Therefore, as important as your physical appearance, our inner physical self (physical fitness) is also vitally important.

Physical fitness is defined as a "state of physiologic well-being that is achieved through a combination of good diet, regular physical exercise, and other practices that promote good health."[9] The following are benefits to being physically fit (in shape):

- Weight loss and weight control
- Reduces the risk of disease (Heart, Diabetes, and some cancers)
- Strengthens your muscles and bones
- Gives you energy and improves your ability to be more active

- Improves your mental health and mood
- Builds confidence
- Improves physical appearance, makes one feel and look more attractive

Our bodies are the temples of the Lord and the vehicles that we navigate through this earthly existence; therefore, we are required to be good stewards with our bodies.

So far we have considered the emotional, financial and physical components of the self. Let us now consider the spiritual self.

Spiritual Self

The ultimate relationship should be with Christ! Before you give yourself to anybody, else I highly recommend you give yourself to Christ. Your relationship with Christ should be a priority. Jesus instructed his disciples to, "Seek ye first, the kingdom of God and all his righteousness and all these things will be added unto you!" (Matt. 6:33)

A couple of years ago, I eulogized a childhood friend, Marvin "Dino" Gordon. Dino was a fun loving brother, with an infectious personality. He was an all-around great guy! I loved to hear him laugh. The last few months of his life, Dino became optimistic about his future. The last time Dino and I were together, he shared that he thought he had a call on his life! He felt as if God was calling him into the ministry, not in a traditional sense, but a call nonetheless, to serve. As Dino was about to leave, he said, "Pastor, I'll be back as soon as I get myself together!" He then gave me a handshake, a hug and left. That was the last time I saw Dino alive.

The first and final words of a man are the most powerful and potent. Dino's last words to me were, "I'll be back as soon as I get myself together." This is called procrastination, putting off things that should have been done long ago for tomorrow. I believe there are some of you who are reading this book that may have said the same thing or feel the same way in saying:

As soon as I get myself together . . .

I'll go back to school.
I'll get married.
I'll start going to church.

We procrastinate and put off making a commitment until tomorrow! We postpone the inevitable, trying to hold on to the moment! Additionally, we also put off or postpone doing the right thing until tomorrow. We act as if tomorrow is promised to us.

Dino said, "as soon as I get myself together, then I'll be back." Unfortunately, Dino never made it back. Don't miss the message. The time to get yourself together is now! "Yet you do not even know what tomorrow will bring. What is your life? For you are a mist that appears for a little while and then vanishes." (James 4:14)

Quit putting off important things that should be done yesterday until tomorrow. Quit ignoring the present. We need to have a sense of urgency in our lives. We need to live like we know we are dying.

That project you've been putting off—Do it now!
That doctor appointment you've been putting off—Do it now!
That apology you've been putting off—Do it now!

Finally, let me say to you what I wish I would have said to my brother Dino: the only way to get yourself together is through having a relationship with Christ Jesus!

Ever since I decided to follow Jesus, I have felt such a significant difference in my life, and I'm not alone; I've seen Jesus transform so many lives. As they entrust their lives to Jesus, and begin to turn and follow Him, they experience countless benefits. Some are extreme examples of transformation such as: leaving immoral lifestyles and destructive addictions, as well as criminals becoming productive citizens. Others have had more subtle shifts and changes, but the benefits and good that come to them by living out the gospel is vivid and astonishing!

There are so many benefits of following Jesus. Here are just a few:

1. You feel the weight of sin and shame lifted. There is an immediate effect of believing and receiving Christ—the sensation of the weight of sin and shame being lifted are completely removed from your heart and mind. It is not something anyone has to make up or explain to you. As you put your trust in Jesus and His gospel, and ask Him to forgive you for your sins, you can literally feel His forgiveness. (Rom. 8:1)

2. You sense the power of sin is broken. Sin and destructive patterns lose a great part of their luster once you believe in Jesus and receive Him into your life. Sin (i.e., temptation to do things contrary to God's word) is still there, and Christians are not perfect, but ultimately, we don't crave it like we used to. The craving only goes away, when you are no longer engaging in your previous sinful activity and realize that there is no temptation given to men, that God will not provide a way of escape. (1 Cor. 10:13)

3. God is with you. God promises in the gospel that He will not only forgive and cleanse you, but he will also be with you. There is instant access, when you trust in Jesus, to the presence and glory of God. As you worship, pray, read the Scripture, walk in Christian community, you will sense that you are not alone. And never will be again.

4. Restored family and relationships. One of the powerful effects of the gospel is that it saves you from allowing your life to revolve around yourself. God shows and empowers you in the cross how to pick up your own cross and live like Jesus did.

5. See God's activity in your life. As your eyes open to the greatness of Jesus in the gospel, you will begin to take notice of God's grace and activity in your life in profound ways. You no longer relate and question a "God out there somewhere," but instead you know that He is here, He is near, and He is at work in your life in mind boggling ways.

All of this is available to every human being on earth through the Gospel. God loved you so much that He sent His one and only Son to pay the sacrifice for your sins on the cross. He did this because you and I are not good enough on our own. Believe in what God has done for you, and begin to trust your life to Him and experience these countless benefits! [10]

Steps Toward Salvation:

1. Confess the Lord Jesus Christ as your personal Lord and Savior. (Rom. 10:9–10)
2. If you haven't been baptized, get baptized. (St. Matt. 28:16–20)
3. Join a bible teaching and practicing church and become an active part of that community of believers. (Acts 2:41–47, Rom. 12:1–2).

Note: Every church has its own process for membership.

Prayer of Repentance and Salvation:

Dear Lord Jesus,

I am a sinner in need of salvation. Please forgive me for all my sins. I acknowledge you and accept your grace and salvation. Thank you Lord. AMEN

Congratulations, if you prayed that prayer welcome to the family of God. You are now saved from eternal damnation! As soon as possible, please join a Bible teaching and preaching church where you can be nurtured and developed in the faith.

Once you have matured emotionally, financially, physically, and spiritually by making a conscious decision to follow Christ, you are now ready to be in relationship with others. Let's now consider the type of relationship known as **friendship i**n Chapter Two.

Self-Reflection Questions:

1. What is the one thing that makes you special or unique?
2. How do you think people perceive you or what have you been told about the way you are perceived to others?
3. If money were not a constraint, what would you be doing with your time?
4. What are you grateful for?
5. If you die tomorrow, will you be happy with the life you've lived?
6. If someone made a movie out of your life, what would it be like?
7. In one paragraph, describe yourself?
8. Reflect back over your life, are there any regrets?
9. Make a list of people that you have wronged in your life. How could you correct those wrongs?

TWO

Friendship

❦

Ecclesiastes 4:9–10 and Amos 3:3

"Rare is true love, true friendship is rarer?"

— Jean De La Fontaine

RELATIONSHIP TIP #4:

"Before you become anything else, become friends!"

In the 80's a popular rap artist, Whodini wrote a song called *Friends*. Like the title suggests, the song is about friendship. Here is a verse and the chorus of the song.

Verse 1:

"Friends Is a word we use everyday

Most the time we use it in the wrong way

Now you can look the word up, again and again

But the dictionary doesn't know the meaning of friends

Chorus:

Friends, how many of us have them?

Friends, ones we can depend on

Friends, how many of us have them?

Friends, before we go any further let's be friends"[11]

I agree with Whodini; before you go any further, you should be friends.

Contrary to popular belief, the first step in a relationship is not lovers, but friends. Friendship is the ideal place to start any relationship. Unfortunately, the starting point for many is lust rather than friendship.

Recently I heard a true story of a successful young woman who went to a nightclub and met a guy. On the surface they both were really attractive people and they were attracted to each other. They seemed to be compatible. She was a successful executive and he was a highway patrolman. They left the club and went back to her condo. They had an evening of lust and sex. After one night, she thought that he was the one for her. In her mind she had found her husband. Within a week, she invited him to move in with her and he did. However, the more they got to know each other and their real personalities, the less attractive they were to each other. What started out great, fizzled out rather quickly. Shortly thereafter she died of a massive heart attack. Those closest to her suggest she possibly died of a broken heart. Perhaps all of this could have been avoided and maybe a life saved if, they would have taken the time to get to know each other through the vehicle of friendship.

In relationships it is not wise, nor necessary to go from ground zero to the top all at once. Take your time and get to know each other. Take time to determine and to discover whether or not you like what you are lusting after or attracted to. Never confuse lust with like or love. Lust is a physical attraction and enticement. Lust has an expiration date. Lust and looks fade.

So what does lust look like and how do you know when you are in lust and not love? Dr. Helen Fisher suggests you know that you are in lust when:

1. You're focused on the physical appearance of the object of your desire.

2. There is a strong desire to have sex, but not deep emotional conversations.
3. You'd rather keep the relationship on a fantasy level, not discuss real feelings.
4. You are lovers, but not necessarily friends.

According to Dr. Fisher, lust can transition into love, but it takes time. It happens when the two really see each other (their strengths and weakness) and get past the fantasy level.[12] This revelation and knowledge is established and solidified during the friendship stage.

Friends are Gods' gift to humanity. Friends are our traveling buddies and our companions on this journey called life. Friends are there to improve the quality of our lives, they are with us through the best and worst of times.

My mother once gave me some great wisdom on selecting a life partner. She said, "Son, if you cannot imagine them there at the gravesite with you when your parents or loved ones pass away; or if you can't imagine them there with you on the worst day of your life, they are not the one!"

You'd be surprised that it is not a lack of love, but a lack of friendship that makes unhappy marriages.

I believe that friends are our partners in the struggles of life. Solomon, the writer of Proverbs says that two can accomplish and achieve more than one. (Eccles. 4:9) It's true we are much more powerful together than we are by ourselves. My good friend Clarence Stowers, the Pastor of the Mars Hill Baptist Church in Chicago puts it this way, "We can go further [and] faster, together." Meaning we make more progress and reach our goals through collaboration and companionship.

Additionally, friends are there to support us! Solomon, "If one falls, the other pulls him up; but if a man falls when he is alone, he's in trouble." (Eccles. 4:10) Recently during a leadership-training workshop, we did a team building exercise, called the Trust Fall. The Trust Fall game is used to build community, teamwork, and trust within the group as members are forced to rely on the protection of the others to prevent themselves from being injured. It was interesting to see how members of our leadership team responded (participated) or in some cases didn't respond to the game. Here is what I learned from the Trust Fall game, if you don't trust people, you will not blindly fall into their arms. In order to successfully play the game, you must trust those with and behind you. If you don't feel safe and secure or that the person you are with has your back that is a relational red flag (proceed with caution). For example, consider the incident between Tony and Annette.

Tony and Annette had been dating for a couple of months, when he decided it was time for Annette to meet his circle of friends. Tony invited his friends to meet them at a nightclub in his old neighborhood. On the way to the nightclub, Annette expressed how excited she was to meet Tony's friends and that she was glad he was taking her to meet them. Tony explained that before they went to the next level in their relationship, it would be important for her to know where he came from. By meeting his friends, she could better understand who he was.

They finally made it to the club. The atmosphere was electric. As they made it to the table, Tony's friends begin to embrace him and give him a lot of love. Tony then introduced Annette to all of his friends. They all embraced Annette and then sat down to begin what would seem to be an amazing night of new beginnings. They began to do shots of tequila.

At first everyone seemed to be getting along, but as the night progressed and Tony's and his friends continued with the shots of tequila, the crazier the night became. Tony and his friends were drunk, talking loud and getting rowdy. Annette became uncomfortable and expressed her concern to Tony and asked to leave. However,

Friendship

Tony was not ready to go. Annette had never seen this side of Tony. Annette began to withdraw from the activities and conversation. One of Tony's friends, Jaq, observed Annette's disposition and begin to try to engage Annette and then intercede on Tony's behalf. But Annette was not feeling it. She wanted to go. Then Jaq began to verbally attack Annette saying, "You think you are better than us? You too good to drink with us?" You are just a stuck up B." Annette got up from the table and went to the car and Tony went after her.

The tension in the car was so thick, that you could cut it with a knife. Tony decided to break the ice, by asking Annette, "What's wrong with you?" Tony's question, only made Annette angrier and she begin to cry. Tony asked her, "Why are you crying?" Annette responded, "I'm crying because I'm mad and I'm hurt." Tony asked, "Why are you mad and hurt?" Annette said, "I'm mad and hurt because your friend Jaq is a jerk. I'm mad because he disrespected me. But I'm hurt because you didn't defend me. You let him disrespect me, which is unacceptable. As your girlfriend, I would expect you to defend me. But you said nothing. To add fuel to the fire, you don't even know or think you did anything wrong! I cannot be with a man who doesn't respect or protect me." This is a great example of how security gone awry within the confines of a friendship or courtship could quickly change the nature thereof or even end the relationship.

It's important to feel safe and secure in your relationship. The word 'secure' is from the Latin word *se,* meaning without, and *cure,* meaning fear. Secure therefore means without fear. The two places you should always feel safe and secure are in your home and within your relationships.

The friendship process also helps to determine compatibility. You must be equally yoked. The prophet Amos asked, "Can two walk together, except they be agreed?" (Amos 3:3) It's important for us to understand that agreement does not always mean approval or consent. Agreement has more to do with alignment and support. In fact friends disagree all the time. But at the end of the day they have to find a way to make it together. There are many ways to get where you're going, but the journey is much more enjoyable when everybody in the car is willing to go the same way.

Friends will enhance one another's life! Solomon is correct, when he proclaimed, "Iron sharpeneth iron; so a man sharpeneth the countenance of his friend." (Prov. 27:17)

I am fortunate to have two best friends, my wife Veneeta and Donald Montgomery. They both have profoundly enhanced my life. I could not imagine my life or where I would be without them. They have seen and been there for me at my best and worst moments. What I love about both of them is that they have loved me unconditionally, even when I haven't been so loving and faithful to them, in spite of my imperfections, they still love me. I am blessed to be called their friend.

The following friendship characteristics are taken from Ellen Bean's online article entitled, *11 Characteristics of a Friend:* [13]

- **Accepting.** A true friend accepts you as you are. They will not try to change you or ask you to be somebody you are not.
- **Dependable.** A true friend is dependable and you can count on them. They will not abandon you in times of need or crisis. They stick with you in good and bad times.
- **Honest.** A true friend will be honest with you and will tell you the truth. They don't lie just to spare your feelings.
- **Listener.** A true friend always listens to you and cares about your needs and emotions. Avoid friends who always have to be the center of attention and monopolize the conversation.
- **Understanding.** A true friend respects your privacy. They understand that you have a family, other friends and colleagues who are part of your life too. I will say this again: avoid people who want to monopolize and control your time.

- **Trustworthy.** A true friend does not gossip about you or talk behind your back. A true friend is a person you can trust and won't say anything about you or try to damage your reputation. They don't talk about you and they don't let other's talk about you.
- **Secure.** A true friend never gets jealous of your success, but would be happy for you.
- **Supportive.** A true friend is supportive of you and your goals.
- **Giving.** True friends give more than what is asked. They share and they give. They have a generous spirit.
- **Loving.** A true friend loves you unconditionally. They know all about you. They know your secrets and your imperfections and they still love you.

My grandmother, Mother Eleanor Keys, was right when she said, "Friends are few and far between. If you have one good friend in your life, consider yourself fortunate."

RELATIONSHIP TIP: #5

A friend is someone who knows all about you and still loves you.

Concerning friendship, Dutch Catholic priest, theologian and writer, Henry Nouwen, once said,

> When we honestly ask ourselves which person in our lives mean the most to us, we often find that it is those who, instead of giving advice, solutions, or cures, have chosen rather to share our pain and touch our wounds with a warm and tender hand. The friend who can be silent with us in a moment of despair or confusion, who can stay with us in an hour of grief and bereavement, who can tolerate not knowing, not curing, not healing and face with us the reality of our powerlessness, that is a friend![14]

RELATIONSHIP TIP: # 6
"Choose your friends wisely. Don't install and maintain a friendship revolving door in your life."

One of my favorite poems entitled, "Friendship," suggests, "Friendship is a plant of slow growth. Trust only those who you know and has shown you that they care."[15] Unfortunately the word friend, just like love, is a very misunderstood and misused concept or idea. Throughout your life there will be many who come in and out of your life. Friends come in many capacities: there are seasonal, short term, and even long term friends.

I recently reconnected with my college roommate DC Randle after thirty years. I had not seen DC since my wedding. During our reunion lunch, DC said to me "although I haven't seen you in thirty years, it feels like we've never missed a beat." We clicked and reconnected.

Although, it's debatable how great a friend I've been to DC and vice versa, based upon our lack of communication. However, there is no doubt in my mind that we are friends; brothers beloved and there is nothing that we wouldn't do for each other. Hopefully in the next thirty years, we will do better with communication and visiting each other.

The closer we get to the end of life, the more important family and friends become. I agree with Pastor Rick Warren, who writes in *The Purpose Driven Life,*

> "I have been at the bedside of many people in their final moments, when they stand on the edge of eternity, and I have never heard anyone say, "Bring me my diplomas! I want to look at them one more time. Show me my awards, my medals, that gold watch I was given." When life on earth

is ending, people don't surround themselves with objects. What they want around them is people—people they love and have relationships with.

In our final moments we all realize that relationships are what life is all about, and wisdom is learning that truth sooner rather than later. Don't wait until you're on your deathbed to figure out that nothing matters more." [16]

Once you have gotten yourself together and have established a solid friendship foundation, the next thing to consider is level of compatibility.

Friendship Reflection Questions:[17]

1. What characteristics do you value most in a friend?
2. How would you rate yourself as a friend?
3. Is the person you are dating or married to, your friend?
4. If you are in a sinking ship with everyone you know, and you could only save ten people, who would you save?
5. If you die today, who do you think will miss you the most?
6. What do you think they will they say in your eulogy?
7. What do you expect out of your friends?

THREE

Equally Yoked!

2 Corinthians 6:14–17 *and* **Deuteronomy 22:10**

"I don't care how intelligent or attractive someone is,

if he zaps your energy, he isn't for you.

True chemistry is more than intellectual compatibility.

Beyond surfaces, you must be intuitively at ease."

— Judith Orloff

RELATIONSHIP TIP: #7

Compatibility counts.

Anyone considering a romantic relationship should be clear as to who they are, what they need, and more importantly what type of person they are most compatible with. The following story underscores the importance of self-knowledge and compatibility. On a first date, a young man once asked a young lady the following question;

"What kind of man are you looking for?" She sat quietly for a moment before looking him in the eye and asking. "Do you really want to know?" Reluctantly, he said, "Yes."

She began to expound, "As a woman in this day and age, I am in a position to ask a man what he can do for me that I can't do for myself. I pay my own bills. I take care of my household without the help of any man. I am in the position to ask, 'What can you bring to the table?'"

The man looked at her. Clearly he thought that she was referring to money. She quickly corrected his thought and stated, "I am not referring to money. I need something more." I need a man who is striving for perfection in every aspect of life." He sat back in his chair, folded his arms, and asked her to explain.

She said, "I am looking for someone who is striving for perfection mentally because I need conversation and mental stimulation. I don't need a simple-minded man.

I am looking for someone who is striving for perfection spiritually because I don't need to be unequally yoked . . . believers mixed with unbelievers is a recipe for disaster.

I need a man who is striving for perfection financially because I don't need a financial burden.

I am looking for someone who is sensitive enough to understand what I go through as a woman, but strong enough to keep me grounded.

I am looking for someone whom I can respect. In order to be submissive, I must respect him. I cannot be submissive to a man who isn't taking care of his business. I have no problem being submissive . . . he just has to be worthy. God made woman to be a helpmate for man. I can't help a man if he can't help himself."

When she finished her spiel, she looked at him. He sat there with a puzzled look on his face. He said, "You're asking a lot." She replied, "I'm worth a lot."[18]

Again, this story underscores the importance of self-knowledge and compatibility. I highly recommend having similar discussions as early as possible with those whom you would like to have a romantic relationship with. The insight gained from having that type of discussion is critical for determining compatibility and whether or not you should continue to pursue the relationship with that individual.

Compatibility counts. We are living in a day where compatibility is being pushed to its limits. Recently I was in LA visiting my son David. He took me to Roscoe's Chicken and Waffles, yes their specialty is chicken and waffles, together! I have to admit, I was skeptical about that combination. But when you eat them together, it is rather tasty. Strangely enough, it works. I get it, sometimes opposites attract and you are tired of the same old thing and you want to try something new. Variety adds spice to life they say, but there are some things that just don't go together!

In Deuteronomy 22:10 Moses says, "Thou shalt not plow with an ox and an ass together." There is no ambiguity in this text; it is clear, concise, and straight to the point. Moses makes it perfectly clear to the Children of Israel, that when plowing in the field, do not yoke or connect two incompatible animals together.

Physically speaking, connecting the two beasts of burden just would not work. They have two different temperaments and can't communicate. And because they speak different languages, they can't get along. If you yoke them together, eventually the ox will kill the ass, because they are incompatible.

You and I must also be careful yoking up with those who we are incompatible with—compatibility matters. It has been said that opposites attract, and they do, but in order to co-exist, they must find a way to complement each other.

Why is compatibility important? Because incompatible relationships can be very painful, a waste of your time, and a delay to your destiny. Beloved, you have a destiny (A place or places that God is taking you to). You have a purpose (A reason for existing or living). Therefore, all your major decisions must be made in light of your destiny and purpose. Your decisions will either push you towards your destiny or away from it. So you must be prudent or wise when making decisions. You must be deliberate and intentional in every decision you make and every relationship that you pursue. You cannot afford to be callous or cavalier in your relationship decision-making.

There are some things you just can't do because if you do, you will jeopardize your destiny and compromise your integrity. There are some people that you can't be romantically or platonically connected to or in covenant (married or committed to) with, because to do so will also jeopardize your destiny or your kingdom assignment. You must have some standards and be very careful of the company you keep.

I shall never forget the first and last time I learned that lesson. The first time, I was ten years old. A childhood friend and I, who was also a neighbor, got permission from our parents to get ice cream from Baskin Robbins. We rode our bikes to 1st and Roosevelt Road, which was about two miles away from our homes. After we finished eating the ice cream, my [friend] talked me in to going to the Zayres (a department store), which was right next-door. While in there, unbeknownst to me, my friend stole some dog chains. The irony here was that neither he nor I had a dog! As we were leaving the store, the store detective detained both of us. They stripped searched us and discovered that my friend had shop lifted the dog chain. Before we were taken to the Maywood Police station, I protested by saying that I didn't do anything wrong; to which the policeman and detective said to me, you are guilty by association. You were with him, so therefore you are potentially an accessory to the crime. I was scared to death, but I learned the importance of watching the company I keep.

The next memorable experience came during my senior year in college. I was asked by someone very close to me to spend Christmas dinner with them and some more friends. While en route to dinner, they asked me to make a stop. Unbeknownst to me, they were going to score some drugs. As soon as they got back in the car,

The Chicago Police blocked us in and demanded that we get out of the car. There were two policemen, one was white and the other was black (I state their race here because it played a vital role in my thinking about race matters.) They first frisked us and then they searched my car. They found drugs on the passenger side of the car. We were immediately handcuffed and put in the back seat of the squad car.

As I sat in the back seat of the police car, I was heart broken and crushed, because although I knew they had a drug issue, I would have never thought they would do that around me, not to mention put drugs in my car.

As soon as the police got in the car, I began to plead my case. I told him, I was home from school on Christmas break, visiting my family. I informed him that I did not do drugs and didn't have a clue where the drugs came from. The person I was with sat in silence.

Then the black policeman told me to shut up. He said to me have you ever heard of "birds of a feather flock together?" However, the white policeman said, "Son since the car is yours, everything we found in it technically belongs to you. But I believe your story. Therefore, I'm going to let you go. But I'm taking your friend in! We saw him cop the drugs." And what he said after that, I shall never forget. He said, "You need to be careful who you ride with and who you let in your car. I could take you in, but having this on your record could mess you up for life. So I'm going to give you a break today. Merry Christmas!" He let me go and I drove away thanking God for favor and freedom.

That day I learned the following lessons: ignorance is not an excuse for breaking the law and was reminded that people are people and that every white policeman wasn't out to get me and every black policeman wasn't for me either. But the main lesson I learned is that you have to be careful whom you associate with, because the wrong association could derail your destiny.

In the New Testament, in 2 Corinthians 6:14, Paul admonishes the church; "**Be ye not unequally yoked together with unbelievers.**" A yoke is a steering or controlling mechanism for a beast of burdens (working animals like oxen, donkeys, or horses). A yoke is used for control and power. It is especially designed to have two similar species of animals go in the same direction for productivity sake. Paul understands that God can get more done for the kingdom, if people of God connect and create a covenant with other believers who are going in the same way at the same time.

Therefore, Paul strongly recommends to the Christians at Corinth not to be yoked to or in relational covenant/commitment with unbelievers. In other words, do not make a relational commitment with non-believers. Do not connect to those who have no faith in your God, or those who do not pray to your God, read your Bible and believe what you believe. Paul doesn't say this and I know I may be pushing the proverbial envelope here, but; I believe it's important to connect with people who believe in your God and who believe in you! If they don't have any faith or confidence in you, they won't support what you are about or what you are becoming. Never connect with people that can't or won't help you reach your God-given destiny.

Spiritually speaking being unequally yoked has more to do with alignment and assignment, than it does assets. It has more to do with direction and destiny, than it does demographics (where you are from, where you live, work, your education, your net worth, what side of the fence you are from). However, this is where we usually hang our hats, when having this relational discussion, we usually discuss compatibility in these terms:

- *Are we financially compatible?*
- *Are you employed or not?*
- *How much money do you make?*
- *Are we intellectually compatible?*
- *Are we maturely compatible?*
- *Are we socially compatible?*

Paul's issue was not cultural, financial, intellectual, or emotional. His issue was spiritual compatibility. This requires asking some additional questions like:

- *Are you saved?*
- *Are you a member of a church? How often do you go?*
- *Do you read the Bible? Do you attend Bible study?*
- *Do you pray?*
- *Do you tithe?*
- *Do you have children? How is your relationship with them?*
- *How is your relationship with your parents?*
- *Who are your friends?*

During Paul's time men and women's roles were clear; there was no confusion there. The man was the primary breadwinner and was expected to be the spiritual leader of the household. As a result of war, migration, immigration and integration, their world became a melting pot. Resulting in the creation of a cultural and social gumbo, where any and everything was acceptable. And unfortunately it was attractive to the church at Corinth. This integration caused problems, because when they connected with someone, they brought their beliefs, culture, and behaviors with them. Ultimately, whoever is the strongest will influence their direction and destiny.

As believers we are to be "choosey" and "particular." This is not being discriminatory, but rather discriminating! Discriminating is usually used and viewed in a negative light as in being prejudiced or having racial bias, but here I'm attempting to use the word discriminating in a positive light, meaning to recognize a distinction; differentiate or to be selective. When Paul says, do not be unequally yoked, he is really talking about spiritual alignment and assignment. In other words, you both should be going in the same direction to help you fulfill your purpose through Christ.

God saved you and kept you around, because he has something greater for you. Eyes have not seen, nor ears heard, what God has in store for you. You have oxen potential, don't mess it up by getting hooked up with a donkey!

RELATIONSHIP TIP #8:
"Although opposites attract, it is far better to wait for and be with those with whom you are spiritually, emotionally, intellectually, and financially compatible.

Dating an immature, broke, and ignorant heathen is not in your best interest nor in GOD's plan for your life!"

I have learned through the years that most people like or love what they want, however, what we want is not always what we need. It's ok to have a "type," "preference," and "requirements list," and you should, but make sure your "list" lines up with God's will and design for your life.

RELATIONSHIP TIP #9:

"Never be so desperate for companionship and company that you don't do your due diligence. Always pre-qualify and check references!"

Relational due diligence is very important, because it will save you time and heart break in the long run. When V and I were going to buy a house, the realtor asked us to prequalify with a mortgage company. I asked him why and he said: "First of all, to determine how much house you can afford and secondly, so that you don't waste my time or yours!" This principle applies to relationships too. Always pre-qualify. Never be so desperate for companionship and company that you don't do your due diligence. Additionally, pre-qualification is necessary for your heart's protection. Consider the case of Pam and Gerald.

Pam and Gerald met and fell in love and became inseparable. They spent a lot time at Pam's house. Pam figured since Gerald was always there, he might as well move in. Pam offered and Gerald accepted the offer and moved in after two weeks of dating. About one month after moving in with Pam, Gerald proposed and Pam said yes. For some reason, they wanted to get married within two weeks. So they came to me and asked me to perform the wedding. I said to them that it is my custom to do a minimum of three pre-marital counseling sessions before I marry a couple. They pleaded their case, by saying both had been married before, didn't see the need for counseling and therefore didn't make it a priority. Due to the short timeframe to get married, I decided to modify my best practice and condensed the pre-marital counseling sessions from three to one.

We had the pre-marital session the day of the wedding rehearsal. During the session, some issues from their previous marriage began to surface. As Pam began to ask questions, about his previous marriage, Gerald became very angry and stormed out. I went after him to try and calm him down, so that we could continue. He came back and we continued, but did not deal with the deep issues and concerns of his past marriage. This was definitely a red flag for me and should have been one for them too!

The next day, against my better judgment, I married Pam and Gerald. It was a beautiful wedding and everything went off as planned. Pam and Gerald were married.

Four months later, Pam called to inform me that she had filed for a divorce and that she was leaving the church. I was saddened by the news. She said, "He wasn't who I thought he was. After the wedding he began to change. Gerald and I were not compatible."

I felt really bad. In retrospect, I firmly believe that had we done our due diligence during the pre-marital counseling session, maybe I could have helped to save their marriage—or prevented them from getting married in the first place. One of the purposes and benefits of thorough pre-marital counseling is its ability to reveal relational red flags.

As a result of that situation, I made a promise to myself: not to marry a couple that would not submit to pre-marital counseling sessions and complete the pre-marital counseling homework[19]. Pre-marital counseling helps with the prequalification process. I highly recommend that anyone considering getting married should submit to pre-marital counseling. If your pastor or wedding officiate doesn't offer pre-marital counseling, please find a certified marriage counselor to perform this service, because it is well worth the investment.

You and I are worth a lot! As Christians, we are to be the temple of the living God. Therefore, we cannot afford to go polluting, profaning or desecrating ourselves, by consistently giving our pearls to pigs (Matt. 7:6). In other words, don't waste your time with those who don't know your value or who don't know how to protect, progress, pray for, or preserve you!

Compatibility Reflection Questions:

1. Am I ready to be in a romantic relationship?
2. Describe your ideal mate?
   a. Prepare a list of attributes that you prefer.
      1. Prioritize them. What are your top five?
3. What characteristics or attributes are a turn-off for you?
4. What are the relationship non-negotiable(s) for you?
5. Does what you want in a mate agree with who you are and how God made you to be? If so, how? And if not, how not?
6. Have you had a failed relationship? If you have, why didn't it work out?

Reflections of our Journey Together Down Through the Years

Futher, Faster, Together

Wedding Date November 22, 1986

Wedding Day, November 22, 1986

Reflections of our Journey Together Down Through the Years

Wedding Party

Kenneth and Veneeta at the wedding reception

Futher, Faster, Together

Kenneth and Veneeta on the beach in Maui, Hawaii

Cruising

Reflections of our Journey Together Down Through the Years

Pastor's Anniversary

Futher, Faster, Together

Veneeta and Kenneth on Graduation Day June 2, 2102, from Northern Seminary

FOUR

Cut Ungodly Soul Ties!

1 Corinthians 6:16

"When we have sex with somebody, we form soul ties—bonds that can tie us emotionally and spiritually to someone else."

Unknown

Frank and Vickie met in high school and quickly became an item. They were high school sweet hearts and inseparable. After prom and graduation, most students went their separate ways, but Frank and Vickie were determined to have a love that would last forever.

Frank was a sought after athlete with athletic scholarship offers and decided to go to school in Wisconsin. Meanwhile, Vickie decided to stay close to home and go to the local community college. They tried to make it work, but a long distant relationship was not really in the cards for either one of them. After a while, they decided to go their separate ways.

Frank graduated from college and eventually got married, but he never forgot about Vickie. Similarly, Vickie moved to California, met a nice guy, and got married, too, but she never forgot about Frank.

Fast-forward twenty years, Frank is now divorced and Vickie is happily married for more than twenty years. One day while surfing Facebook profiles, Vickie stumbled upon Frank's profile, sent him a message and decided to try and befriend him.

At first Frank and Vickie's social networking reconnection seemed innocent. Their relationship went from the occasional liking and commenting on statuses and pictures, to chatting and sending personal messages on a daily basis. To them it seemed as if they were back in high school, and eventually they planned a private reunion.

What made this reunion possible? What was the driving force? Was it Facebook? Was it social networking? Or perhaps the connection and driving force behind their reunion was a soul tie.

By definition a soul tie is:

> A spiritual connection between two people who have been physically intimate with each other or who have had an intense emotional or spiritual association or relationship.[20]

The concept of soul ties can be found in 1 Corinthians 6:16. "What? know ye not that he which is joined to an harlot is one body? for two, saith he, shall be one flesh." In this text, Paul is really not focusing on the morality of prostitution per se. He is focusing more on the joining or tying together of two people (souls) through sexual intercourse outside of the institution of marriage. In Genesis 2:24, Moses uses similar language, "Therefore shall a man leave his father and his mother, and shall cleave unto his wife: and they shall be one flesh." Here this scripture is referring to the Godly soul tie that happens at the consummation of marriage. Again, during the sexual act, the two (souls) become one flesh (soul tie).

Soul ties are differentiated into two categories: Godly soul ties, such as those that normally develop between a husband and wife (Gen. 2:24), and ungodly soul ties (1 Cor. 6:16), such as those that are said to be caused by premarital sex, adultery, various kinds of abuse, and occult activity.

Negative Soul Ties need to be cut or broken.

RELATIONSHIP TIP #10:
Cut the Soul Ties

Ungodly soul ties that are not broken or cut, can lead to relational and emotional problems. Therefore, any ungodly soul tie needs to be cut; which is the best advice for how to affair-proof your relationship.

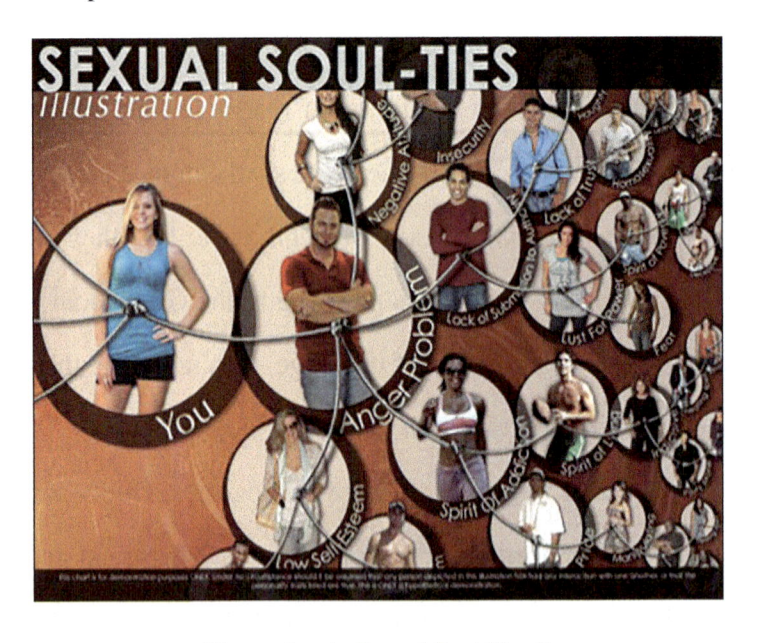

Illustration A: Sexual Soul Ties.[21]

From the illustration one can easily see the interconnectedness of soul ties. You may not realize it, but every person you have sex with, deposits and leaves a part of their soul in you. That's why causal sex is not ok because in doing so, you might ignorantly connect with a destructive temperament or proclivity. Anybody can be good for a day, but just give them some time and the real person will eventually emerge. Ultimately, you don't want a soul tie with someone that has destructive tendencies.

For those who have already made those connections, you've got to break the soul tie. It must be properly dealt with and disposed of or it will come back to haunt you! They will find you on Facebook, Twitter, LinkedIn, or any other social media outlet. They may even track down your cell phone or email, show up at your job, your home or text you in the middle of the night, when you are most vulnerable and lonely. You've got to get rid of the soul tie.

The following tips on how to Break Soul Ties were taken from MinisteringDeliverance.com. [22]

How to Break Soul Ties:

"Step #1:

Repent of any sins that involve that person.

You need to know soul ties are more than just physical connections; they have emotional and spiritual dimensions. Therefore, you have to confess and repent of the sins you have committed with them. It is vital that you repent of those sins and receive God's forgiveness before you can break the soul tie.

Step #2:

Forgive the person of any wrongs done.

Unforgiveness forms an unwanted unhealthy connection to your past. "If you have any unforgiveness in your heart against the person, you must choose to release that bitterness and forgive the person. The Bible is clear that bitterness defiles a man."

Step #3:

Renounce any covenants made with the person.

If you have made any spoken commitments, vows or even simply saying, "I will love you forever," it has ample power in the spiritual realm to bind the soul to that person (form a soul tie). The tongue is quite capable of binding the soul and can be a great means to create soul ties."

Renounce and break the soul tie in Jesus' name.

There is power in the name of Jesus! To renounce means, "to give up by formal declaration" and "to repudiate; disown."[23] Verbally renouncing something carries a lot of weight in the spiritual realm. Just as vows can bind the soul, renouncing can release the soul from bonds. Jesus said that whatsoever you shall loose will be loosed in heaven (the heavenly realm, or spiritual realm). You can renounce and loose yourself from an ungodly soul tie by simply speaking something like this from your heart:

"I now renounce and loose myself from any ungodly soul ties formed between myself and _____, and I break these ungodly soul ties in Jesus' name."

Step #4:

Get rid of any gifts exchanged.

Gifts also symbolize a relationship and can hold a soul tie in place. If a person has a ring, personal gifts, cards, jewelry, and other 'relationship gifts' from a previous relationship, get rid of them. Remove and destroy anything holding or connecting you to that person. I would strongly recommend, throwing away all material items that connect you to that person (e.g. cards, letters, clothes, watches, shoes, furniture, sexy garments, etc.). Those tangible items symbolize the ungodly soul tie that you have with that person. You must break free and begin to purge these things from you in the natural. Holding on to those things symbolizes that the relationship is still in good standing and can actually hold the soul tie in place even after it has been renounced."

Cut the soul ties today!

Soul Ties Reflection Questions:

1. What is a soul tie?
2. How is a soul tie formed?
3. How to break a soul tie?
4. How can you avoid soul ties?

FIVE

Become Relationship Custodians

Leviticus 25:3

"When it comes to relationship maintenance, consistency is key."

Unknown

I went to college in the small farming town of Waverly, Iowa. During my time there, I got a chance to learn a little about farming and to see the process of sowing, reaping, and crop rotation first hand.

Crop rotation is a process of systematically rotating or planting of different crops on the same land for the benefit of improving soil fertility.[24] During the Old Testament biblical era, God instructed Israel to prune the crops every six years, allow the land to rest on the seventh year and begin farming the land again during the eighth year. Israel did so for soil maintenance. The soil had to be good, in order that the crop would remain healthy and grow. So it is with relationships, in order for it to grow, we have to be wise stewards who are committed to the relationship maintenance process! If you don't invest in and maintain your relationship, it will not grow or yield the best relationship possible.

Every relationship needs to be maintained, but many of us neglect to take the time to do so. There are many ways that healthy relationships can be maintained.

First you must examine the relationship and decide whether it is growing healthy, reached a plateau, or declining. Additionally, you must decide if the relationship still works for you or the other person. This type of introspection is called a collective assessment. Meaning, both of you need to assess how "we" are doing? You have to do more than just look at the relationship from your perspective. You have to also consider the other person. Within your relationship don't assume just because "YOU are good, that WE are good!" Every now and then you have to ask the question, "Are we good?" "How are we doing?" You've got to ask, "Is it still good to you?" In addition to asking the question, you must also assess or observe interaction, attitude and behavior. If you and your spouse or significant other are not talking to one another, something is wrong! If you can't seem to get along and are always fighting, something is wrong! If you are married and you all are now sleeping in different rooms in the house or different homes, something is wrong! In addition to maintenance, every relationship needs healthy lines of communication.

Every relationship needs communication. It is important to keep the lines of communication open and intact. Broken communication will kill a relationship. This involves both talking and listening and more importantly, validating your understanding of what you hear! This is vitally important, because it is dangerous to operate in ignorance or with misunderstanding.

Unfortunately, as a society, we need to be taught, and in some cases re-taught, how to listen, so that we can truly hear. In order to listen you must do the following;

1. **Pay attention when someone is talking, don't multi-task.** If you are already formulating a response while you are reading or someone is speaking, you are not listening.
2. **Always validate your understanding, before you respond to what you think you heard.** I have found that far too many people have what is called guarded listening; meaning that we process what people are saying through filters that can sometimes make us miss the message.

Finally, if you see or feel something is wrong, check it out and, if possible, fix it! Recently I was watching a controversial episode of Iyanla: Fix My Life on the OWN network.[25] During this episode Iyanla was assisting two gay pastors and their families come to grips with their homosexuality and empowering them to share their secrets with their congregations and loved ones. One of the pastors was married and as a part of the process, Iyanla interviewed his estranged wife. During the interview Iyanla asked the wife, "When did you first notice something wasn't right with your relationship?" She replied, "About five or six years ago." Iyanla then asked, "So you have been living with the pain and hurt all this time? You've been keeping this to yourself all this time? Why didn't you say something?" The pastor's wife visibly checked out of the conversation. She shrugged her shoulders and dropped her head. Then Iyanla said, "Look at me! Emotions buried alive never die, they fester and stink and bleed." I agree with Iyanla. Perhaps some of the pain and suffering that she (and he) endured could have been avoided if when they first noticed there was a problem in the relationship, they would have done something about it. This is a very common problem with relationships. Never assume things will fix themselves. Because if you let it go too long, things might become irreparable! When you see something, say something. Communicating what's wrong must be followed up with corrective action. If you don't know how to fix it, get some professional help! See a Christian counselor ASAP!

How to Take Your Relationship to Another Level

Recently I was having difficulties with my MacBook Pro, it was slow, sluggish and often crashed in the middle of performing critical tasks; therefore, I took it back to the manufacturer, Apple. While speaking to the service tech, he told me "For optimal performance of your MacBook Pro, you must apply regular software updates and perform maintenance from time to time. However, to improve performance, the following steps are recommended." Likewise with relationships, in order for the relationship to work properly, regular checkup and maintenance is required.

The following tips are recommended to improve or enhance the relationship.

- **Date often.** *Even if you don't have money, find ways to befriend and romance each other. Date frequently, and put it on the calendar, as this is sacred time.*
- **Leave little notes.** *Leave sticky notes in the bathroom, kitchen, office or car.*
- **Send just because cards or texts.**

- *Write a poem.*
- *Send a plant or an Edible Arrangement.*
- *Do a random act of love or service—just because!* Here are a few ideas: cook a special meal, have a candlelight dinner, make breakfast and serve it in bed, have a picnic lunch outside, do something you don't normally do, that you know they would love for you to do. (NOTE: If you are looking for things to do, just search your memory bank for requests made that have been going unfulfilled. Nagging and complaints can serve as great opportunities and material for random acts of love or service).

All in all, those are a few ways that you can take your relationship to the next level.

Couple's Reflection Questions

The following are marriage maintenance questions from Tom and Jeannie Elliff. Tom and Jeannie encourage married couples to ask these questions every year in order to keep their marriage sharp. [26]

QUESTIONS HUSBANDS CAN ASK THEIR WIVES

1. What could I do to make you feel more loved?
2. What could I do to make you feel more respected?
3. What could I do to make you feel more understood?
4. What could I do to make you more secure?
5. What could I do to make you feel more confident in our future direction?
6. What attribute would you like me to develop?
7. What attribute would you like me to help you develop?
8. What achievement in my life would bring you the greatest joy?
9. What would indicate to you that I really desire to be more Christ like?
10. What mutual goal would you like to see us accomplish?

Optional: Have I overlooked any question you would like me to ask?

QUESTIONS WIVES CAN ASK THEIR HUSBANDS

1. Do you feel I properly understand the goals that God has placed in your heart? How can I help you achieve them?
2. What are some things I can do to regularly show you just how satisfied I am with you as my husband and the leader of our home?
3. Is there anything I am doing or failing to do that seems to send a signal that I do not honor you or your leadership in our home?
4. Is there anything I can change to make our home a place where you feel more satisfied and comfortable?
5. Are there any big dreams in your heart that you have been hesitant to share with me? How can I help you fulfill them?
6. How do you feel we can begin communicating better than we already are?
7. Do you feel that there is anything keeping either one or both of us from God's best in our lives? What should be my part in freeing us from those restraints?
8. Are we where you wanted us to be at this stage in life? How can I help you make that possible within God's guidelines?
9. How do you envision our future together? What can we do together to achieve that goal?
10. What can I do to show you how much I need and trust you?

SIX
Exit Strategy

St. Matthew 21:18-21

"If you are brave enough to say good bye,

life will reward you with a new hello."

Paulo Coehlo

If we are honest, we've all been in relationships that went on or lasted long past their expiration date! You may be right there now. There is something within each of us that is a hopeful romantic. We want love to last forever. That's why songs like Heat Wave's, *Always and Forever* or Anthony Hamilton's, *I Can't Let Go* resonate with us.

But I have discovered that no relationship is meant to last forever. There is a beginning and ending to everything. The Ecclesiastical author King Solomon is correct, there is a time, a season, and a purpose for every relationship under the sun! But the question is, how do you know when the relationship is over?

To help in determining when a relationship is over, let us consider Jesus' teaching in St. Matthew 21:18-21, the cursing of the fig tree. As Jesus was heading towards His destiny to die on the cross for the sins of the world, He was hungry and decided to stop at a fig tree to get some breakfast.

According to the scripture, "Now in the morning, as He returned to the city, He was hungry. And seeing a fig tree by the road, He came to it and found nothing on it except leaves" (Matt. 21:18,19).

That's just like Popeye's, Church's Chicken, or Kentucky Fried Chicken running out of chicken. Imagine what you would do or say if you were hungry and you drove to your favorite fast food restaurant, the sign says that they are open, the lights are on, there are people in the store and behind the counter; but they don't have anything to sale or serve!

Jesus, in his wisdom, saved others from despair and disappointment by cursing the fig tree and causing it to die! Jesus said, "Let no fruit grow on you ever again" and immediately the fig tree withered away (Matt. 21:19).

Why did Jesus perform such a damning and "destructive" miracle? Don't miss this point—As you get closer to your destiny, relationship consideration and examination is critical, you don't have time to play games. The closer you get to your destiny, the more picky and discerning you have to be. The older you get, the more you have to become a choosy lover. Everyone is not anointed or ordained to go with you into your promised land! This is sad to say, but some people who are with you now, will not make it with you when you get to your destiny. This might seem cold, but here is the reality. Jesus had a real need. He went to a place that should have been able to provide his need, but He found nothing on it but leaves. Essentially, the tree was a picture of "false advertising," having leaves, but no figs. This should not be the case with these particular fig trees, which customarily did not bear leaves apart from figs. Let me ask you a question. Have you ever met someone who professed to be something that they were not? Or have you ever met anyone that said that they could do "A-Z," but could not even do "A"? That's false advertising. In a relationship, you don't want someone who falsely advertises all the leaves and has no fruit. When you are hungry or you have a substantial need, leaves just won't do! You want and need someone that can produce (bear fruit)! Let me put it another way. You need to minimize the amount of non-productive people in your life. If they are not bringing anything to the table, already invested or investing in you, the project or task at hand, don't give them unlimited access to your head and heart! Because to do so is a losing proposition for you right from the start! It is not in your best interest to keep company with non-productive people.

Jesus' encounter and interaction with the fig tree shows us how we too can know when things are over and how to respond accordingly.

From the text, you know it's over when one or more of the following conditions occur:

1. *The relationship is no longer being productive or is not currently bearing fruit or signs of life.* Meaning they are all talk, but no action. The relationship is just a "tale told by an idiot, full of sound and fury, signifying nothing." [27] However, this more than just feeling or not feeling it any more. This is about no fruit, because sometimes you just "don't feel" each other; but that doesn't mean it's over. It just means you aren't feeling each other at the time. "Not feeling each other," is more of a warning or an indicator that maintenance is needed. Therefore, a mature relationship must go beyond feelings.

2. *After you talk about it (over and over and over again), and the relationship still refuses to grow or shows any*

evidence of life! You know it is over when they no longer respond to you!

3. *When the relationship ceases to exist or begins to misrepresent what you and God intend or need for it to be!* In other words, they have changed into something that you no longer recognize or respect.

4. *Abandonment or unauthorized leave of absence.* This is when one or the other in the relationship goes A.W.O.L. (Absent Without Leave). No rhyme or reason just leaves the relationship without communicating the fact that the relationship is over.

5. *No respect for each other or the relationship.* When you lose respect for the person, your marriage or exclusive relationship, that's a warning sign the relationship, is on life support.

As aforementioned, a preoccupation with dead things is really not healthy for you. When I was an intern chaplain at the MacNeal Hospital in Berwyn, IL, I was brought to the emergency room to counsel a pregnant woman who had been carrying a baby for almost nine months. The woman was sick and near death. However, when they examined her, they discovered that the fetus was the problem—she was carrying a dead baby. The doctor's told her, if she wanted to live, they would have to remove the dead fetus. The only problem was she didn't want to do it. For she loved her unborn baby and had great hopes for its life, and now she was informed that it was dead! I was called in to comfort and counsel this mother. After much discussion and prayer, eventually she elected to have the doctors remove the dead fetus. It was difficult, but if she hadn't done it, she would have died too.

Many people seem to have the hardest time parting with or letting go of dead things. We just don't know when to let go, but the truth is, some relationships and habits need to be cursed and buried. I know sometimes letting go is hard, but supporting a dead relationship is emotionally and mentally draining. If the relationship is dead, it needs to be cursed and buried.

Reflection Questions

1. What is your relationship producing?
2. Do you spend more time loving or fighting (arguing)?
3. Are the two of you heading in the same direction?
4. Is your spouse or significant other responding to you?
5. Do you listen to each other?
6. In what ways do you honor and respect each other?

SEVEN

Let's Stay Together

Ecclesiastes 4:9–12

Jack and Charlotte had been married for thirty-five years. They were empty nesters: a few years away from retirement. From the outside they appeared to be living the American dream, they seemed to have it all. Until one day they woke up and decided they could no longer do this. But prior to separating, they decided to make one final attempt at salvaging the marriage and agreed to see a certified marriage counselor.

At the counseling session Charlotte burst into tears and declared, "Well it wasn't really all of a sudden, we've been stuck in a rut for some time. And I just decided to fake it until we made it!" "What do you mean Jack asked?" Charlotte said, "I think George Benson says it best and she began to quote the lyrics from his song, Masquerade:"

Are we really happy here/ With this lonely game we play/ Looking for words to say/ Searching but not finding understanding anywhere/ We're lost in a masquerade/ Both afraid to say we're just too far away/From being close together from the start/We tried to talk it over but the words got in the way/ We're lost inside this lonely game we play/To understand the reasons Why we carry on this way/We're lost in a masquerade[28]

Like Jack and Charlotte, there are some marriages and relationships that are lost in a masquerade; wearing the mask of happiness, to keep up public perceptions. But beneath the mask, they are really struggling to keep their relationship together. Relationships in general are under satanic attack, especially marriages.

I read an article recently, entitled *Top 10 Reasons Marriages Fail*.[29] According to the writer of the article, here are the top ten reasons most marriages fail.

1. **Financial Problems**
2. **Communication Problems**
3. **Family Problems**
4. **Sex Problems**
5. **Friend Problems**

6. **Addiction Problems**
7. **Abuse Problems**
8. **Personality Problems**
9. **Expectation Problems**
10. **Time Problems**

My order and category differs, as to the most common problems I've seen in relationships and why they fail. What I have observed is that communication is the number 1 reason why relationships fail. Here is my top ten list of why most relationships fail:

1. Communication—Communication problems occur for several reasons and range from not talking to each other, talking at each other, to talking over one another. These problems also include: not listening, misinterpreting or misunderstanding each other. I spend a lot of our time together coaching the couple in communication skills. Usually once we strengthen the lines of communication, this empowers the couple to deal with most of the other issues on this list.

2. Infidelity—Infidelity or cheating leads to broken trust. Infidelity impacts several areas of the relationship, especially the area of intimacy. Unless one is able to forgive and trust again, the relationship doesn't have a chance once infidelity occurs.

3. Finances—Money matters involve debt, money management, and unemployment. In most cases whoever has the most money, has the most power and controls the relationship. That's why most couples prefer their own money (accounts, etc.) and the wealthy often require a prenuptial agreement.

4. Intimacy—Sexual issues in the relationship can include lack of intimacy, sexual incompatibility, impotence, and/or addiction to porn.

5. Time Management—Time related issues are usually related to not making the relationship a priority.

6. Abuse—Relational abuse occurs in many forms; verbal, sexual, mental, emotional, and physical. Abuse in any form has no place in a relationship and should not be tolerated.

7. Expectation—Expectation issues occur when one or the other fails to live, love, or serve up to the other's expectation. I agree with Lauren Hill who says, "Unfulfilled expectations are the mother of disappointment."

8. Outside Influence—This involves anyone who negatively impacts the relationship that is outside of the primary couple.

9. Growth—Change issues occur when one or both parties involved in the relationship grow apart. This is usually the result of failing to grow together.

10. Incompatibility—Incompatibility happens when the couples' core values, preferences or interests are not compatible. It only becomes a problem when the couple cannot resolve their differences (often called irreconcilable differences).

Again, healthy lines of communication would prevent most of the above relationship issues on both lists from occurring.

At the end of the day, the only couples that stay together are the ones that want to stay together. Staying together is not an easy task.

This involves having the courage to face your issues, forgive one another (and self) and keeping the relationship real and relevant. Therefore, when R&B Legend Al Green, wrote a song entitled "Let's Stay Together" he described the epitome of what it takes to maintain a relationship. The chorus says "Let's, let's stay together/ Lovin' you whether, whether/ Times are good or bad, happy, or sad!" As believers in Christ, I firmly believe, we should make a conscious choice to stay together. My In-laws, Anne and Dan "Pops" Brewster were married for fifty-six years. During that time Pops would often say, "We have been married so long, that if she leaves, she's going to have to take me with her, cause I'm leaving too!" Ultimately, marriage is covenant and a commitment that you choose to be a part of.

Why should you consider staying together? First, we should stay together because two people are better off than one! In other words, we are much better together than we are apart! If we are separate we are vulnerable and susceptible to attack! But when we come together we are undefeatable! The passage of scripture in Ecclesiastes captures the sentiments best in saying that:

> Two people are better off than one, for they can help each other succeed. If one person falls, the other can reach out and help. But someone who falls alone is in real trouble.

Likewise, two people lying close together can keep each other warm. But how can one be warm alone? A person standing alone can be attacked and defeated, but two can stand back-to-back and conquer. (Eccles. 4:9–12) New Living Translation (NLT)

A few years ago, my dental hygienist shared with me a story that underscores the point the Ecclesiastical writer is trying to make. At the time, she was recently divorced and living alone in the country. One day, while out walking her dogs alone without her cell phone, she accidently stepped into a hole, twisted her ankle, and broke her leg. The injury was so painful, that she could not move and just laid there for a while. She screamed for help, but no one could hear her. Her closest neighbor lived over a mile away. Finally she decided to crawl back to the house to call for help. It took her over an hour to crawl back to the house. She said to me, "It's moments like that, that I wish I would have stayed married or at least lived with someone that could have helped me when I fell." Not only should we stay together because two are better than one, but we should stay together for strength and help. We should also stay together for closeness and intimacy. I agree with Herbert Anderson and Freda A. Gardner, in their book entitled, *Living Alone,* who asserts "To be human is to be in relationship with others."[30] In order to stay together you must have a made up mind and resolve to: forgive, love each other, agree to disagree, pray together, and work together. Earlier in the chapter I mentioned an older couple, Jack and Charlotte who were going through some marital issues after being empty nesters for years. While it is true that Charlotte seemed to have a despondent attitude towards Jack and described it to him by using the first verse of George Benson's classic hit "Masquerade," Jack's response shocked both Charlotte and the counselor. His only reply to Charlotte was, "baby you missed a part of the third verse which goes like this—"Thoughts of leaving disappear/ Every time I see your eyes/ No matter how hard I try!"

Jack and Charlotte's story is a model for those in a troubled relationship. If you are willing to fight for the relationship, you can stay together. There is hope. All is not lost when those involved really want to make it work.

EIGHT

Forgiveness — The Greatest Gift

Matt 6:12–15

"The weak can never forgive.
Forgiveness is the attribute of the strong."

Mahatma Gandhi

Human beings are relational creatures. We need company and companionship; just like we need food and water, we need others to survive. To be in relationship with others, is to risk hurt and sometimes hurting others and being hurt. You must understand that being in relation to and with others, one person will offend and the other person will encounter offence; so on a daily basis, we need to pray, "Father forgive us our debts as we forgive our debtors."

God's remedy for relational hurt and broken trust is FORGIVENESS. In my last book, entitled *Made in His Image*[31], I asserted that forgiveness is never about them, it's always about you. You don't forgive because they deserve it; you do so because you deserve it.

Not only is forgiving others tied to our being forgiven, but there are also other benefits to forgiveness:

- *Forgiveness makes reconciliation and restoration possible.*
- *Forgiveness lowers stress, reduces ulcers, migraines, and other stress related disorders.*
- *Forgiveness is good for your heart—literally.* One study from the *Journal of Behavioral Medicine* found forgiveness to be associated with lower heart rate and blood pressure as well as stress relief.

With all of the benefits and blessings that come from forgiving, why is it so hard to forgive?

REASONS PEOPLE DO NOT FORGIVE

1. Denial Some people feel they don't have issues with other people, nor do people have issues with them. It's been my experience that we all, from time to time will either offend or be offended. All you have to do is tell someone no and they might be offended. It is possible to have an issue with a person and not be aware of it!

2. *Refusal* When we are offended, we want justice and we want it now! There is an innate internal need to have people pay for what they have done to us. We want revenge, retribution, and reprobation. We may also think that to forgive is to let them get away, when getting away is not an option.

But the interesting thing is that, the same person that wants justice also loves mercy and grace! Thank God we don't always get what we deserve!

3. *Memories* Forgiveness does not erase one's memory. You can forgive, but unfortunately you will never forget, unless you want to. God is not asking you to forget it, nor is he asking you to act as if it never happened. However, with the help of the Lord, it is possible for the painful memory of the offense to no longer have a hold or impact on us. With the help of the Lord, we can disassociate the pain, anger, and hurt.

4. Definition Many are afraid that the definition of forgiveness means reconciliation or restoration of relationship. However, forgiveness is not guaranteed to lead to restoration or reconciliation. It can, but it is not a requirement. You can forgive and not restore! Reconciliation and restoration is an option or benefit that forgiveness makes possible. But it highly possible to forgive and not get back together. You can forgive and not return to the same level of relationship again—and that's ok.

5. Release Forgiveness by definition is to release from debt, that's it and that's all. Reconciliation and restoration are added graces, only made possible, through the generosity of those who have been offended. Therefore, one must think twice before one acts and engages in harmful behavior to those they are in covenant with. An apology or tears, no matter how sincere they are, may not remove the consequences of one's actions. The consequences that follow is the prerogative of the victim.

6. Uninformed Many people do not forgive, because they don't know how. They haven't been taught how to forgive.

When I was little, if I offended my loved ones and my mother was there, she would always make me say, "I'm sorry." or "Apologize." But I don't remember being taught, what to do when someone offended or hurt me. The rule of thumb that I followed was to get mad and get even. Forgiveness is not innate; it's a conscious choice and learned behavior.

Regardless of the reasons for not forgiving, Unforgiveness, grudges, and unresolved issues hinder your prayer life. (Matt. 6:15) Unforgiveness makes it virtually impossible for God to do supernatural miracles in your life. The forgiven must be willing to also forgive, otherwise it impairs your relationship with God. If we think of unforgiveness in terms of the following example, I believe we will think twice when we want to choose to harbor grudges.

One Sunday, while preaching a message on forgiveness, I enlisted the assistance of two talented and athletic young men in our congregation. I gave them an empty bag and asked them to walk around the sanctuary with the bag on their shoulder. Initially the bag was empty and walking was easy, but as they continued to walk, I added weights (the weights were in different denominations, representing sins and offenses) to the bag. The more I added the more difficult it became for them to carry the bag. In fact, they started sweating and struggling to carry the bag. A couple of times they sat down and finally they decided to drop the bag. I asked them, "Why did you drop the bag?" They replied, "Because it was too heavy to carry."

Please understand the point I am making. Everywhere we go, we carry an invisible bag with us. We can't see it, but it is there, because we can feel it. Inside these bags are issues and offenses (i.e., lying, selfishness, broken promises, cheating, stealing, jealousy, etc.) that we choose to carry or bear.

It's in our best interest to drop our offenses. Time to let them go!

If you are holding on to past hurts and pains . . .

LET IT GO!

If someone has angered you . . .

LET IT GO!

If you are holding on to the thought of evil and revenge . . .

LET IT GO!

If you have a bad attitude . . .

LET IT GO!

If you are stuck in the past . . .

LET IT GO!

If you are struggling with the healing of a broken relationship . . . Forgive and be forgiven.

The way to purge these feelings is to forgive those that have committed these offences against you.

Do yourself a favor, forgive now! You can do that by praying the following Psalm.

Psalm 51

1 Have mercy upon me, O God, according to thy lovingkindness: according unto the multitude of thy tender mercies blot out my transgressions.

2 Wash me thoroughly from mine iniquity, and cleanse me from my sin.

3 For I acknowledge my transgressions: and my sin is ever before me.

4 Against thee, thee only, have I sinned, and done this evil in thy sight: that thou mightest be justified when thou speakest, and be clear when thou judgest.

5 Behold, I was shapen in iniquity; and in sin did my mother conceive me.

6 Behold, thou desirest truth in the inward parts: and in the hidden part thou shalt make me to know wisdom.

7 Purge me with hyssop, and I shall be clean: wash me, and I shall be whiter than snow.

8 Make me to hear joy and gladness; that the bones which thou hast broken may rejoice.

9 Hide thy face from my sins, and blot out all mine iniquities.

10 Create in me a clean heart, O God; and renew a right spirit within me.

11 Cast me not away from thy presence; and take not thy holy spirit from me.

12 Restore unto me the joy of thy salvation; and uphold me with thy free spirit.

13 Then will I teach transgressors thy ways; and sinners shall be converted unto thee.

14 Deliver me from bloodguiltiness, O God, thou God of my salvation: and my tongue shall sing aloud of thy righteousness.

15 O Lord, open thou my lips; and my mouth shall shew forth thy praise.

16 For thou desirest not sacrifice; else would I give it: thou delightest not in burnt offering.

17 The sacrifices of God are a broken spirit: a broken and a contrite heart, O God, thou wilt not despise.

18 Do good in thy good pleasure unto Zion: build thou the walls of Jerusalem.

19 Then shalt thou be pleased with the sacrifices of righteousness, with burnt offering and whole burnt offering: then shall they offer bullocks upon thine altar.

AMEN

Forgiveness Application

Forgiveness is a powerful concept and tool that God has given us to bring peace and reconciliation to our world and relationships. In order to learn to forgive, you must practice it. The following is a forgiveness exercise that I have used with great success.

Directions: Prayerfully consider and complete each step.

Step 1. Pray and ask God to reveal to you any unconfessed sins, unforgiveness, grudges, or resentments in your heart.

Step 2. Write down names. As He reveals them, write them down. Be specific. Write down names, when, what, how often, and a description of the offense.

Step 3. Prioritize them. Note your top three instances or people that you have not forgiven.

Step 4. For the top three, write a forgiveness letter. (Note: You are not to do anything with the letter other than write it at this step. Do not give this letter to them. This step is only for you.) The letter should have the following components:

a. Greeting.

b. Statement of purpose for writing.

c. Description of what happen from your perspective.

d. How it made you feel and how it has impacted your life.

e. Statement of release or forgiveness.

Step 5. Forgive. Forgiveness options: These are things you can do with your letter.

a. Nothing/Save it.

b. Burn it.

c. Tear it up.

d. Throw it away.

e. Mail it or give it to the person.

Step 6. Let it go and move on.

FINAL THOUGHTS

Genesis 12:1–4

"Sometimes you have to let loved ones go and say goodbye."

During the writing of this book, V and I lost our dad, Deacon Dan Brewster, my relationship mentor and the patriarch of the family, whom I affectionately called "Pops." During the memorial services, held at the Jerriel Baptist Church in Cincinnati, Ohio, V shared a very touching story about the nature of their relationship and his character. She shared that in 1990, when we moved to Chicago, the first Sunday being there was very difficult for her. She was homesick, so she called her dad that morning at 7:30 a.m. and they talked. Their conversation made her feel better. The next Sunday, at 7:30 a.m., the phone rang and it was Pops. They talked for a while and he caught her up on the week's activities at home in Cincinnati. Basically he talked and she listened. Then when he got done, he would say, "Alright, gotta go" and then hang up. This

Sunday morning call went on faithfully until he went home to be with the Lord in November of 2014. No matter where she was in the world, V would get a call from Pops, every Sunday morning at 7:30 a.m. It's been months now since Pops left us, and we still can't get used to idea of not receiving that Sunday Morning wake-up call or hearing his voice.

Transition of any kind is difficult but death and relocation of a loved one can be extremely hard on the caregiver and the family at large. Not only did we lose Pops during the period of writing this book, but my family also experienced the loss of our family dog, Redd Foxx and the relocation of our youngest son, David. David's relocation was extremely hard to adjust to for us all, because letting go and saying goodbye is difficult. But it is also part of life and necessary for progress. As David was leaving, he texted the family and said, "Love you guys. I'm going to make you guys proud out here, I promise!" Then he posted the following quote from Neale Donald Walsch on Facebook, which gave me comfort and peace about his leaving. It really did put things into perspective for me, and therefore, apropos to end this book.

"Life begins at the end of your comfort zone."[32]

Final Thoughts

In Loving Memory of Deacon Dan Brewster

Deacon Dan Brewster

ABOUT THE AUTHOR

Rev. Dr. Kenneth D. Phelps, M Div., D.MIN.

Entrepreneur, Community Leader, Pastor, Teacher, Author, and Playwright

Throughout our lives we are often compared to many things and our sincere desire is that these representations are vividly illustrated with positive images that flatter our actions, desires, and achievements. Godly men and women are likened in the Scriptures to sturdy trees and like the tree, Dr. Kenneth D. Phelps, from the pulpit stands straight for God to use him as a teacher, shepherd, and protector. A director of deliverance, this is a man who firmly believes in nurturing his flock by providing spiritual guidance and direction, to those willing to receive it. Amongst the congregation, he is known as mentor, friend, partner, and pastor. In times of delight or despair, he shines as a light of hope exemplifying the glory of God's infinite wisdom through strong convictions and confidence in Christ. He exemplifies the verse "He shall be like a tree planted by the rivers of water, that bringeth forth his fruit in his season" (Ps. 1:3).

Concord Missionary Baptist Church (CMBC) is the fertile valley in which Dr. Kenneth D. Phelps thrives and grows in grace. He confessed Christ at an early age, licensed to preach in November 1990, and ordained as a Minister of the Gospel in May 1994. His life-long relationship and devotion to the Lord manifested itself in Dr. Phelps being elevated to the position of a pastor. He received and accepted the call to pastor CMBC on December 19, 1994.

Dr. Phelps is also owner and CEO of IMANI Faith Productions, Inc., which is a faith based media production company. Additionally, Dr. Phelps is the founder / CEO of Concord Community Organization, which is a non-for profit 501c3 organization designed to bring peace to Woodlawn community in Chicago, IL.

Not only is Dr. Phelps an accomplished minister of the gospel, but he has been employed with the Lexis Nexis company for twenty-eight years. He is currently employed as a Lead Field Systems Engineer where he is responsible for leading the Midwest U.S. and Southern U.S. team of Field Systems Engineers.

Finally, Dr. Phelps is the author of several papers, books, blogs and devotions:

About The Author

- *Made in His Image* Xulon Press (2002)
- *30 Day Journey to Forgiveness Devotional* IMANI Faith Productions Publications (2008)
- *Restoring Congregational Health Through Discipleship and The Implementation of the Small Group Process at the Concord Missionary Baptist Church of Chicago, IL* (Thesis) (Northern Seminary © Kenneth D. Phelps, 2012)
- *Further, Faster Together; Godly Advice to Foster a Deeper, Long Lasting and Meaningful Relationship.* Xulon Press (2015)

Married for twenty-nine years to Veneeta B. Phelps, Dr. Kenneth D. Phelps is the father of three beautiful children who are his pride and joy: Kenneth, Morgan, and David. He is a grandfather to Kalissa Destiny Harlan.

Dr. Phelps holds a B.A. in Computer Information Systems from Wartburg College, a Master of Divinity, and a Doctorate of Ministry degree from Northern Baptist Theological Seminary.

APPENDIX A

Premarital Counseling Sample Questions:

1. How would you define marriage?
2. Why do you want to get married?
3. Do you love your future spouse? Why?
4. What are three things that you most respect about your future spouse?
5. What are three things that you would like the other to improve upon?
6. Describe your expectations of your spouse?
7. What are the keys or formulas to a successful marriage?
8. How will the finances be handled in the relationship (please consider current indebtedness)?
9. What is your vision for your marriage?
    a. Where do you want to be in your marriage and how do you plan to get there in:

i. one year?

   ii. five years?

   iii. ten years?

10. What are your personal dreams or ambitions? Any career changes ahead?

11. What problems are you encountering now in your relationship?

12. What happens when you get angry?

13. A marital support system is a group of married couples, mentors, spiritual leader/advisor and other family members and friends that are committed to the success and support of your marriage. Describe your marital support system? Is it healthy and intact?

14. What are your thoughts about divorce? If you believe in divorce, what are the conditions or circumstances for divorce?

15. What would happen if you found out your spouse was unfaithful to you (committed adultery)? What would be the consequences?

16. What's your philosophy on raising children?

17. How do you feel about disciplining children?

18. What's your biggest fear about marriage?

19. What role will spirituality/religion play in your marriage?

Appendix A

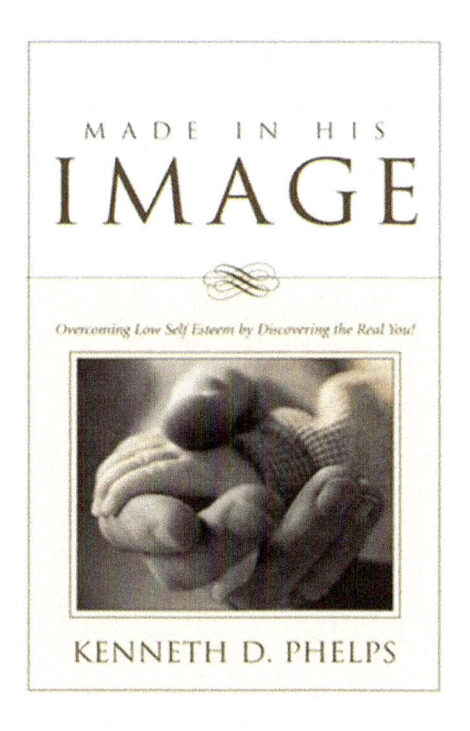

ALSO BY KENNETH D. PHELPS

AVAILABLE AT XULONPRESS.COM OR AMAZON.COM

NOTES

(Endnotes)

Introduction:
1. Hendrikus Berkhof, *Christ Faith: An Introduction to the Study of Faith* (Grand Rapids: Wm. B. Eerdmans Publishing Company, 1991).
2. "Marriage Rate," *Huffington Post,* Accessed August 16, 2014, http://www.huffingtonpost.com/2013/07/22/marriage-rate_n_3625222.html.
3. "U.S. Divorce Rates and Statistics," *Divorce Source,* Accessed May 26, 2014, http://www.divorcesource.com/ds/main/u-s-divorce-rates-and-statistics-1037.shtml
4. Biblical reference Psalm 51:10.
5. Self here is defined as natural human proclivities or carnal or sin nature.
6. Recovery idiom. See http://whatmesober.com/personal-writing-about-addiction-and-recovery/movin-on/as-sick-as-our-secrets/ for details.
7. "Emotions," *Webster Dictionary Online,* Accessed September 2, 2014, http://www.merriamwebster.com/dictionary/emotionshttp://www.thefreedictionary.com/emotion.
8. 360 Degree Feedback, also known as Multi-Rater Feedback, Multi-Source Feedback, or Multi Source Assessment, is feedback strategy usually employed by employers and counselors to obtain feedback for their employees or clients, that comes from members

of an employee's immediate work circle, friends and family. For more on 360 Degree Feedback go to http://www.custominsight.com/360-degree-feedback/what-is-360-degree-feedback.asp.

9. "Fitness," *The Free Medical Dictionary,* Accessed November 22, 2014, http://medical-dictionary.thefreedictionary.com/physical+fitness.

10. "5 Benefits of Following Jesus," *Thinke* (Blog), Accessed November 22, 2014. http://www.thinke.org/blog/2013/5/8/5-benefits-of-following-jesus.html.

Chapter TWO

11. Jalil Hutchins and Larry Smith, Whodini, *Friends,* Vinyl, Jive Records, 1984. Lyrics accessed @ http://www.songlyrics.com/whodini/friends-lyrics/

12. Helen Fisher "How to Tell if its Love or Just Lust," *Mind Body Green,* Accessed October 26, 2014, http://www.mindbodygreen.com/0-12048/how-to-tell-if-its-love-or-just-lust.html.

13. Ellen Bean, "11 Characteristics of a True Friend," *Ellie Bean,* Accessed November 22, 2014, http://elliebeandesign.com/11-characteristics-of-a-true-friend/.

14. Henri J.M. Nouwen, "The Road to Daybreak: A Spiritual Journey,"*Patheos (Blog), Accessed November 22, 2014,* www.patheos.com/blogs/frankviola/afriend/.

15. Author unknown.

16. Rick Warren, *Purpose Driven Life.* (Grand Rapids: Zondervan Publisher, 2002),126.

17.

Chapter THREE

18. Ross Cochran, "Genesis 26:34–35 – INCOMPATIBLE!," *Words Of Life* (Blog), Accessed May 25, 2015, https://pastorross1.wordpress.com/2011/10/13/genesis-2634-35---incompatible/.

19. Pre-Marital counseling questions. Please see Appendix A.

Chapter FOUR

20. "Soul Tie," *Dictionary of Christianese,* Accessed December 22, 2014, http://www.dictionaryofchristianese.com/soul-ties/.

Notes

[21] Shawn and Jennifer Spears, "I'm Free," *ShawnandJenniferSpears.com,* (Blog) Accessed December 22, 2014, http://www.shawnandjenniferspears.com/2014/09/im-free.html.

[22] "Breaking Soul Ties," *Ministering Deliverance,* Accessed December 23, 2014, http://ministeringdeliverance.com/breaking_soul_ties.php.

[23] "Renounce" *Dictionary.com,* Accessed December 23, 2014, http://dictionary.reference.com/browse/renounce

Chapter FIVE

[24] "Crop Rotation" *The Free Dictionary,* Accessed January 5, 2015, http://www.thefreedictionary.com/crop+rotation.

[25] Iyanla: Fix My Life. " Fix My Secret Life as a Gay Pastor: Part 2" Oprah Winfrey Network, September 26, 2015.

[26] Tom and Jeannie Eliff, "10 Questions Every Couple Should Ask Every Year." *Family Life,* Accessed January 5, 2015, http://www.familylife.com/articles/topics/marriage/staying-married/communication/10-questions-every-woman-should-ask-her-husband-every-year#.VTmMryjSnZc

Chapter SIX

[27] William Shakespeare, *Macbeth,* No Fear: Macbeth: Act 5, Scene 5, Page 2, (1611)

[28] Leon Russell and George Benson. *Masquerade* Vinyl, Warner Brothers, 1976.

Chapter SEVEN

[29] "Top 10 Reasons Marriages Fail" *Divorce.com,* Accessed November 23, 2014, http://divorce.com/top-10-reasons-marriages-fail/.

[30] Herbert Anderson & Freda A. Gardner, F. A. *Living Alone.* (Louisville: Westminster John Knox Press).

[31] Kenneth D. Phelps, *Made In His Image.* (Fairfax: Xulon Press, 2002).

FINAL THOUGHTS

[32] Quote By Neale Donald Walsch

CPSIA information can be obtained
at www.ICGtesting.com
Printed in the USA
LVOW01s0745050216
473757LV00003B/3/P